A MID
NIGHT

C000274686

The RSC Shakespeare

A MIDSUMMER NIGHT'S DREAM

Edited by
Jonathan Bate and Eric Rasmussen

With a Foreword by Marc Wootton
and Introduction by Jonathan Bate

palgrave
macmillan

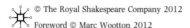
Published 2012 by
MACMILLAN PUBLISHERS LTD
Houndmills, Basingstoke, Hampshire RG21 6XS
Companies and representatives throughout the world

ISBN-13 978-1–13702631–6 paperback

This book is printed on paper suitable for recycling and made from fully managed and sustained forest sources.

A catalogue record for this book is available from the British Library.

10   9   8   7   6   5   4   3   2   1
21   20   19   18   17   16   15   14   13   12

Printed in China

FOREWORD

Marc Wootton

Last year I was lucky enough to be asked to perform the role of Nick Bottom in Shakespeare's *A Midsummer Night's Dream* at the RSC in Stratford-upon-Avon. It has become the highlight of my theatrical career thus far, and to be honest the entire experience still feels like a bit of a dream. The RSC has always held a special place in my heart since witnessing Ian Judge's production of *The Comedy of Errors* when I was just a boy. Incidentally, it starred Desmond Barrit, who in my mind gave us the best Bottom ever!

A Midsummer Night's Dream is an exceptional play. Yes, like all good art it borrows from other sources, but in its entirety it's a real triumph of originality. Testament to its strength can be found in its ability to withstand being continually manipulated by directors. I have been fortunate enough to witness a few of these productions over the years, including Robert Lepage's spellbinding staging at the National Theatre, Gregory Doran's sublime production at the RSC with its hysterical Pyramus and Thisbe, and most recently Sean Holmes' superbly irreverent version at the Lyric in Hammersmith. Each time a kaleidoscope of fresh meanings and images are presented to a new audience. These have been discovered via the many filters the play has passed through in rehearsal, during its journey from the page to the stage.

The immensely intuitive Nancy Meckler, joint artistic director of Shared Experience, was at the helm of our inventive production. Thankfully, the RSC indulged our company with the opportunity to play and investigate the text over several weeks. We began rehearsals by sitting in a circle and taking it in turns to speak a line aloud, offering an explanation of its meaning to the rest of the group. As a writer of comedy I was in awe of how well drawn the characters were and how succinct the writing was. This fascinating process made me aware of the myriad interpretations and choices available to both performer and director. It also intrigued me to see how different genders interpret the same play. Looking back, it's comforting to think how much of this preliminary exploration ended up featuring in our final production. I found Michael Pennington's frank and honest account of the play in his *User's Guide* to the *Dream* a useful accompaniment throughout the rehearsal process and would urge you to get a copy if you want to learn more about the play in performance.

I would never have imagined that rehearsals for a Shakespeare play would feature improvisation so heavily. This really encouraged me as a performer to explore the character and situations extensively. Improvisation relies on trust, and thankfully I was surrounded by a group of supportive performers. It formed a huge part of our rehearsal process and it's a great technique for exploring the characters in a contemporary era. Not only are you able to move away from the rigours of Elizabethan English, but the glorious 'happy accidents' that occur using this method merrily find their way into performance. Our final Pyramus and Thisbe play was littered with such occurrences.

Nick Bottom is a member of the mechanicals, a collective of market traders or workmen in our case, instantly recognizable types whose anxieties are strangely familiar amongst the surrounding confusion of the rest of the play. He's a gift of a part, such a timeless comic character. In my mind, all good comedic characters are delusional and the greater the delusion, the funnier they are. The distance between Bottom's idea of himself and who he actually is creates the space where the comedy lies. However, he's not just plain stupid: despite his bravado he has some incredibly insightful things to say. I've always felt the key to playing any comedic role is about the truth and conviction you employ to realise it in front of an audience. For me, it's vital to remain faithful to the character and never play just for laughs.

I was very nervous about having to show my Bottom and with days to go before performing my interpretation of this iconic character I met with the legend that is David Troughton at the infamous Dirty Duck pub in Stratford-upon-Avon. He gave me some great advice: 'You *are* Bottom, it says so in the programme!' He urged me to clear my mind of other people's versions of the role and trust my instinct and intuition. In the end, that's all we have. And your opinion and interpretation is what defines you. Sadly, within the vast intellectual canon of Shakespeare it's easy to get intimidated by what you are supposed to do, or what it's supposed to mean, rather than what it means to you. It's a tall order but so important that you trust your instincts and ultimately trust the text.

Whilst playing Bottom I received a number of letters from people who had seen our production. Some of my favourites were from children who knew me from the *Nativity* films. I felt so very privileged to feature in their lives for that moment in time and proud to be a gateway into the wider world of William Shakespeare. However, the most gratifying letter I received was from the other end of the age spectrum. An elderly man wrote to say that he had never quite 'got' Shakespeare until he witnessed our production. I must admit, until meeting my wonderfully generous company and the good folk behind the curtain at the RSC, Shakespeare was pretty much lost on me too. It's no surprise then, that my journey mirrors that of Bottom's, for Shakespeare has beautifully defined the whole dramatic process in just a few short scenes. Starting with casting, then performance anxieties, the age-old struggle between creator and actor, through to the practicalities of solving staging and finally, of course, the performance. It's all part of the inspirational voyage the mechanicals go on to discover the true magic of theatre.

If you've read it before then you are only too aware of the delights you have in store and if you are new to it then you are about to embark on a truly unforgettable trip. However, one last bit of advice that often gets overlooked is making sure you speak it aloud. This magical play was meant to be performed; it's not for sitting quietly in the corner and reading. So, get up, find yourself a little space, and speak it!

INTRODUCTION

Jonathan Bate

Shakespeare is the poet of double vision. The father of twins, he was a mingler of comedy and tragedy, low life and high, prose and verse. He was a countryman who worked in the city, a teller of English folktales who was equally versed in the mythology of ancient Greece and Rome. His mind and world were poised between Catholicism and Protestantism, old feudal ways and new bourgeois ambitions, rational thinking and visceral instinct. *A Midsummer Night's Dream* is one of his truly essential works because nowhere else is his double vision more apparent than in this play's movement between the city and the wood, day and night, reason and imagination, waking life and dream.

Wood, night, imagination, dream. These are the co-ordinates of the second form of sight, which is best described as magical thinking. It is the mode of being that belongs to visionaries, astrologers, 'wise women' and poets. It conjures up a world animated with energies and spirit forces; it finds correspondences between earthly things and divine. The eye that sees in this way rolls in a fine frenzy, glancing from heaven to earth, from earth to heaven. It bodies forth the forms of things unknown, turns them to shapes and gives to airy nothings a local habitation and a name.

Magical thinking answers a deep human need. It is a way of making sense of things that would otherwise seem painfully arbitrary – things like love and beauty. An ugly birthmark on a baby would be explained away by the suggestion that the infant might be a 'changeling child', swapped in the cradle by some night-tripping fairy. The sheer chance involved in the process of what we now call sexual chemistry may be rationalized in the story of the magic properties of the juice of the flower called love-in-idleness. And in a world dependent on an agricultural economy, bad harvests were somehow more palatable if explained by the intervention of malicious sprites upon the operation of the weather.

In the age of candle and rush-light, nights were seriously dark. The night was accordingly imagined to be seriously different from the day. The very fact of long hours of light itself conferred a kind of magic upon midsummer night. This is the night of the year when magical thinking is given full rein.

Theseus and Hippolyta never meet Oberon and Titania. In the original performance, the respective roles were likely to have been doubled. The contentious king and queen of fairies thus become the dark psychological doubles of the betrothed courtly couple. The correspondence inevitably calls into question the joy of the match between Athenian and Amazon. Oberon actually accuses Titania of having led Theseus 'through the glimmering night' when he deserted 'Perigenia whom he ravishèd', of having made the day duke break faith with a succession of paramours. Shakespeare loves to set up an antithesis, then knock it down. Here he implies that there is ultimately no sharp distinction between day and night: the sexual ethics of Theseus are perhaps as dubious as those of the adulterous child-possessor Titania.

Authority figures, representatives of the day world of political power, win little sympathy in *A Midsummer*

Night's Dream. For the lovers, the forest may be a place of confused identity, but at least it is an escape from the patriarchal match-making of Egeus. In the audience, the characters with whom we engage most warmly are neither monarchs nor lords, but the mischief-making Robin Goodfellow and the ineffable weaver, Bottom. Each in his way is an embodiment of the theatrical spirit that animates everything that is most gloriously Shakespearean. Always a man of the theatre, Shakespeare lives in a world of illusion and make-believe that hits at deepest truths; he knows that his world is fundamentally sympathetic to those other counter-worlds which we call dream and magic.

Robin the Puck compares the mortals to fools in a fond pageant: he has a right to think of himself as author of the play, since it is his dispensing of the love juice that fuels the plot. As for Bottom, at one level he is a bad actor. In both rehearsal and performance of 'Pyramus and Thisbe', it becomes clear that he does not really understand the rules of the theatrical game. But at a deeper level, he is a true dramatic genius: he is gifted with the child's grace to suspend his disbelief.

As Pyramus, he puts up a pretty poor performance; as Ass, it is another matter. The comical deficiency of 'Pyramus and Thisbe' is that the actors keep telling us that they *haven't* become their characters. The Assification of Bottom is, by contrast, akin to those brilliant assumptions of disguise – Rosalind becoming Ganymede in *As You Like It*, Viola Cesario in *Twelfth Night* – through which Shakespeare simultaneously reminds us that we are in the theatre (an actor is always in disguise) and helps us to forget where we are (we willingly suspend our disbelief). In that forgetting, we participate in the mystery of magical thinking. With Bottom himself, we in the audience may say 'I have had a most rare vision.'

Many members of Shakespeare's original audience, steeped as they were in the New Testament, would have recognized Bottom's account of his dream as an allusion – with the attributes of the different senses comically garbled – to a famous passage in the first Epistle to the Corinthians, in which St Paul says that the eye of man has not seen and the ear of man has not heard the glories that will await us when we enter the

Kingdom of Heaven. In the Geneva translation of the Bible, which Shakespeare knew well, the passage speaks of how the human spirit searches 'the bottom of God's secrets'. Jesus said that in order to enter his kingdom, one had to make oneself as a child. The same may be said of the kingdom of theatre. It is because Bottom has the uncynical, believing spirit of a child that he is vouchsafed his vision. At the same time, Shakespeare himself offers a dangerously grown up image of what heaven might be like: the weaver may be innocent but the fairy queen is an embodiment of sexual experience. The 'virgin queen' Elizabeth was also known as England's 'fairy queen' and the wood in which the action takes place, with its 'nine men's morris' and English wild flowers, is more domestic than Athenian, so there must have been an inherent political risk in the representation of a sexually voracious Titania. Shakespeare perhaps introduced Oberon's apparent allusion to a chaste Elizabeth – the 'fair vestal thronèd by the west' – in order to dismiss any identification of Titania with the real-life fairy queen whom he knew would at some point be a spectator of the play.

The comedy and the charm of the *Dream* depend on a certain fragility. Good comedy is tragedy narrowly averted, while fairy charm is only safe from sentimentality if attached to some potential for the grotesque. Fairies only deserve to be believed in when they have the capacity to be seriously unpleasant. Of course we laugh when Bottom wears the head of an ass and makes love to a queen, but the image deliberately courts the suggestion of bestiality. In Ovid's *Metamorphoses*, Shakespeare's favourite book and the source for the tale of 'Pyramus and Thisbe', people are driven by bestial desires and are rewarded by being transformed into animals. In Shakespeare, the ass's head is worn in play, but it remains the closest thing in the drama of his age to an actual animal metamorphosis on stage.

Ovid was rational Rome's great counter-visionary, its magical thinker. His theme is transformation, the inevitability of change. Book fifteen of the *Metamorphoses* offers a philosophical discourse on the subject, mediated via the philosophy of Pythagoras. From here Shakespeare got many of those images of transience that roll through his Sonnets, but in the *Dream* he celebrates the transfiguring and enduring power of night vision, of second sight.

Night is the time for fantasy and for love, the time in which your wildest hopes may be indulged but your worst nightmares may have to be confronted. The action in the forest fills the space between the betrothal and the wedding celebration of Theseus and Hippolyta. For the young lovers it is also a time-between, the time, that is to say, of maturation, of discovering who they really are and whom they really love. When Hermia and Lysander, Helena and Demetrius emerge after a midsummer night's madness in the wood, they don't quite know what's happened: 'Methinks I see these things with parted eye, / When everything seems double.' And they're not all quite sure if they've finally gained the person they want: 'And I have found Demetrius like a jewel, / Mine own and not mine own.' But on reflection in the cold light of morning, the strangeness of the night has effected a material transformation, leading the lovers to a truer place than the one where they were at court the day before. Perhaps because she is herself a 'stranger', an outsider in the 'civilized' world of Athens, it is the Amazon queen Hippolyta who understands this best:

> But all the story of the night told over,
> And all their minds transfigured so together,
> More witnesseth than fancy's images
> And grows to something of great constancy;
> But howsoever, strange and admirable.

A MIDSUMMER NIGHT'S DREAM

THESEUS, Duke of Athens

HIPPOLYTA, Queen of the Amazons, betrothed to Theseus

EGEUS, an Athenian courtier, father to Hermia

LYSANDER, in love with Hermia

HERMIA, in love with Lysander, but ordered by her father to marry Demetrius

DEMETRIUS, in love with Hermia, though once a suitor to Helena

HELENA, in love with Demetrius

Peter **QUINCE**, a carpenter and leader of an amateur dramatic group, who speaks the **PROLOGUE** to their play

Nick **BOTTOM**, a weaver, who plays **PYRAMUS** in the amateur play

Francis **FLUTE**, a bellows-mender, who plays **THISBE** in the amateur play

SNUG, a joiner, who plays a **LION** in the amateur play

Tom **SNOUT**, a tinker, who plays a **WALL** in the amateur
  play

Robin **STARVELING**, a tailor, who plays **MOONSHINE** in
  the amateur play

OBERON, King of Fairies

TITANIA, Queen of Fairies

ROBIN Goodfellow, also known as Puck, a sprite in the
  service of Oberon

PEASEBLOSSOM ⎫ fairies
COBWEB ⎪ attendant
MOTH ⎬ upon
MUSTARDSEED ⎭ Titania

PHILOSTRATE, an official in Theseus' court

Other Attendants at the court of Theseus; other Fairies
attendant upon Oberon

Act 1 [Scene 1]   *running scene 1*

Enter Theseus, Hippolyta, with others [Philostrate and attendants]

THESEUS Now, fair Hippolyta, our nuptial hour
　　Draws on apace. Four happy days bring in
　　Another moon: but O, methinks, how slow
　　This old moon wanes; she lingers my desires,
　　Like to a stepdame or a dowager
　　Long withering out a young man's revenue.
HIPPOLYTA Four days will quickly steep themselves in
　　　　nights,
　　Four nights will quickly dream away the time.
　　And then the moon, like to a silver bow
　　New-bent in heaven, shall behold the night
　　Of our solemnities.
THESEUS Go, Philostrate,
　　Stir up the Athenian youth to merriments,
　　Awake the pert and nimble spirit of mirth,
　　Turn melancholy forth to funerals:
　　The pale companion is not for our pomp.
　　　　　　　　　　　　　　　　[Exit Philostrate]
　　Hippolyta, I wooed thee with my sword,
　　And won thy love doing thee injuries.
　　But I will wed thee in another key,
　　With pomp, with triumph and with revelling.
Enter Egeus and his daughter Hermia, Lysander and Demetrius

EGEUS Happy be Theseus, our renownèd duke.

THESEUS Thanks, good Egeus: what's the news with thee?

EGEUS Full of vexation come I, with complaint
  Against my child, my daughter Hermia.
  Stand forth, Demetrius. My noble lord,
  This man hath my consent to marry her.
  Stand forth, Lysander. And my gracious duke,
  This man hath bewitched the bosom of my child.—
  Thou, thou, Lysander, thou hast given her rhymes,
  And interchanged love-tokens with my child.
  Thou hast by moonlight at her window sung,
  With feigning voice verses of feigning love,
  And stol'n the impression of her fantasy
  With bracelets of thy hair, rings, gauds, conceits,
  Knacks, trifles, nosegays, sweetmeats — messengers
  Of strong prevailment in unhardened youth —
  With cunning hast thou filched my daughter's heart,
  Turned her obedience, which is due to me,
  To stubborn harshness.— And, my gracious duke,
  Be it so she will not here before your grace
  Consent to marry with Demetrius,
  I beg the ancient privilege of Athens:
  As she is mine, I may dispose of her;
  Which shall be either to this gentleman
  Or to her death, according to our law
  Immediately provided in that case.

THESEUS What say you, Hermia? Be advised, fair maid,
  To you your father should be as a god,

One that composed your beauties, yea, and one
To whom you are but as a form in wax
By him imprinted and within his power
To leave the figure or disfigure it.
Demetrius is a worthy gentleman.

HERMIA So is Lysander.

THESEUS In himself he is.
But in this kind, wanting your father's voice,
The other must be held the worthier.

HERMIA I would my father looked but with my eyes.

THESEUS Rather your eyes must with his judgement look.

HERMIA I do entreat your grace to pardon me.
I know not by what power I am made bold,
Nor how it may concern my modesty
In such a presence here to plead my thoughts:
But I beseech your grace that I may know
The worst that may befall me in this case,
If I refuse to wed Demetrius.

THESEUS Either to die the death or to abjure
Forever the society of men.
Therefore, fair Hermia, question your desires,
Know of your youth, examine well your blood,
Whether, if you yield not to your father's choice,
You can endure the livery of a nun,
For aye to be in shady cloister mewed,
To live a barren sister all your life,
Chanting faint hymns to the cold fruitless moon.
Thrice blessèd they that master so their blood,

To undergo such maiden pilgrimage.
But earthlier happy is the rose distilled
Than that which withering on the virgin thorn
Grows, lives and dies in single blessedness.

HERMIA So will I grow, so live, so die, my lord,
Ere I will yield my virgin patent up
Unto his lordship, whose unwishèd yoke
My soul consents not to give sovereignty.

THESEUS Take time to pause, and by the next new
moon —
The sealing day betwixt my love and me,
For everlasting bond of fellowship —
Upon that day either prepare to die
For disobedience to your father's will,
Or else to wed Demetrius, as he would,
Or on Diana's altar to protest
For aye austerity and single life.

DEMETRIUS Relent, sweet Hermia.— And, Lysander, yield
Thy crazèd title to my certain right.

LYSANDER You have her father's love, Demetrius:
Let me have Hermia's. Do you marry him.

EGEUS Scornful Lysander! True, he hath my love;
And what is mine my love shall render him.
And she is mine, and all my right of her
I do estate unto Demetrius.

LYSANDER I am, my lord, as well derived as he,
As well possessed: my love is more than his,
My fortunes every way as fairly ranked,

If not with vantage, as Demetrius',
And, which is more than all these boasts can be,
I am beloved of beauteous Hermia.
Why should not I then prosecute my right?
Demetrius, I'll avouch it to his head,
Made love to Nedar's daughter, Helena,
And won her soul: and she, sweet lady, dotes,
Devoutly dotes, dotes in idolatry,
Upon this spotted and inconstant man.

THESEUS I must confess that I have heard so much,
And with Demetrius thought to have spoke thereof,
But, being over-full of self-affairs,
My mind did lose it. But, Demetrius, come,
And come, Egeus, you shall go with me.
I have some private schooling for you both.
For you, fair Hermia, look you arm yourself
To fit your fancies to your father's will,
Or else the law of Athens yields you up —
Which by no means we may extenuate —
To death or to a vow of single life.—
Come, my Hippolyta. What cheer, my love?—
Demetrius and Egeus, go along:
I must employ you in some business
Against our nuptial and confer with you
Of something nearly that concerns yourselves.

EGEUS With duty and desire we follow you.

Exeunt all but Lysander and Hermia

LYSANDER How now, my love! Why is your cheek so pale?
How chance the roses there do fade so fast?

HERMIA Belike for want of rain, which I could well
Beteem them from the tempest of mine eyes.

LYSANDER Ay me, for aught that I could ever read,
Could ever hear by tale or history,
The course of true love never did run smooth.
But either it was different in blood—

HERMIA O cross! Too high to be enthralled to low.

LYSANDER Or else misgraffed in respect of years—

HERMIA O spite! Too old to be engaged to young.

LYSANDER Or else it stood upon the choice of merit—

HERMIA O hell! To choose love by another's eyes.

LYSANDER Or if there were a sympathy in choice,
War, death or sickness did lay siege to it,
Making it momentary as a sound,
Swift as a shadow, short as any dream:
Brief as the lightning in the collied night,
That in a spleen unfolds both heaven and earth,
And ere a man hath power to say 'Behold!'
The jaws of darkness do devour it up:
So quick bright things come to confusion.

HERMIA If then true lovers have been ever crossed,
It stands as an edict in destiny.
Then let us teach our trial patience,
Because it is a customary cross,
As due to love as thoughts and dreams and sighs,
Wishes and tears, poor fancy's followers.

LYSANDER A good persuasion. Therefore hear me,
    Hermia.
  I have a widow aunt, a dowager
  Of great revenue, and she hath no child.
  From Athens is her house removed seven leagues,
  And she respects me as her only son.
  There, gentle Hermia, may I marry thee,
  And to that place the sharp Athenian law
  Cannot pursue us. If thou lov'st me, then
  Steal forth thy father's house tomorrow night,
  And in the wood, a league without the town,
  Where I did meet thee once with Helena,
  To do observance to a morn of May,
  There will I stay for thee.
HERMIA My good Lysander!
  I swear to thee, by Cupid's strongest bow,
  By his best arrow with the golden head,
  By the simplicity of Venus' doves,
  By that which knitteth souls and prospers love,
  And by that fire which burned the Carthage queen,
  When the false Troyan under sail was seen,
  By all the vows that ever men have broke,
  In number more than ever women spoke,
  In that same place thou hast appointed me,
  Tomorrow truly will I meet with thee.
LYSANDER Keep promise, love. Look, here comes Helena.
Enter Helena
HERMIA God speed fair Helena, whither away?

HELENA Call you me fair? That fair again unsay.
    Demetrius loves your fair: O happy fair!
    Your eyes are lodestars, and your tongue's sweet air
    More tuneable than lark to shepherd's ear
    When wheat is green, when hawthorn buds appear.
    Sickness is catching: O, were favour so,
    Your words I catch, fair Hermia, ere I go,
    My ear should catch your voice, my eye your eye,
    My tongue should catch your tongue's sweet melody.
    Were the world mine, Demetrius being bated,
    The rest I'll give to be to you translated.
    O, teach me how you look, and with what art
    You sway the motion of Demetrius' heart.

HERMIA I frown upon him, yet he loves me still.

HELENA O, that your frowns would teach my smiles
    such skill!

HERMIA I give him curses, yet he gives me love.

HELENA O, that my prayers could such affection move!

HERMIA The more I hate, the more he follows me.

HELENA The more I love, the more he hateth me.

HERMIA His folly, Helena, is none of mine.

HELENA None, but your beauty: would that fault were
    mine!

HERMIA Take comfort: he no more shall see my face.
    Lysander and myself will fly this place.
    Before the time I did Lysander see,
    Seemed Athens like a paradise to me.

O, then, what graces in my love do dwell,
That he hath turned a heaven into hell!

LYSANDER Helen, to you our minds we will unfold:
Tomorrow night, when Phoebe doth behold
Her silver visage in the wat'ry glass,
Decking with liquid pearl the bladed grass,
A time that lovers' flights doth still conceal,
Through Athens' gates have we devised to steal.

HERMIA And in the wood, where often you and I
Upon faint primrose beds were wont to lie,
Emptying our bosoms of their counsel sweet,
There my Lysander and myself shall meet,
And thence from Athens turn away our eyes,
To seek new friends and strange companions.
Farewell, sweet playfellow: pray thou for us,
And good luck grant thee thy Demetrius! —
Keep word, Lysander: we must starve our sight
From lovers' food till morrow deep midnight.   *Exit*

LYSANDER I will, my Hermia.— Helena, adieu.
As you on him, Demetrius dote on you!   *Exit*

HELENA How happy some o'er other some can be!
Through Athens I am thought as fair as she.
But what of that? Demetrius thinks not so:
He will not know what all but he doth know.
And as he errs, doting on Hermia's eyes,
So I, admiring of his qualities.
Things base and vile, holding no quantity,
Love can transpose to form and dignity.

Love looks not with the eyes, but with the mind,
And therefore is winged Cupid painted blind.
Nor hath love's mind of any judgement taste,
Wings and no eyes figure unheedy haste.
And therefore is love said to be a child,
Because in choice he is often beguiled.
As waggish boys in game themselves forswear,
So the boy love is perjured everywhere.
For ere Demetrius looked on Hermia's eyne,
He hailed down oaths that he was only mine.
And when this hail some heat from Hermia felt,
So he dissolved, and showers of oaths did melt.
I will go tell him of fair Hermia's flight:
Then to the wood will he tomorrow night
Pursue her; and for this intelligence,
If I have thanks, it is a dear expense.
But herein mean I to enrich my pain,
To have his sight thither and back again.   *Exit*

[Act 1 Scene 2]   *running scene 2*

*Enter Quince the carpenter, Snug the joiner, Bottom the
weaver, Flute the bellows-mender, Snout the tinker and
Starveling the tailor*

QUINCE Is all our company here?

BOTTOM You were best to call them generally, man by
    man, according to the scrip.

QUINCE Here is the scroll of every man's name, which is thought fit through all Athens to play in our interlude before the duke and the duchess on his wedding day at night.

BOTTOM First, good Peter Quince, say what the play treats on, then read the names of the actors, and so grow on to a point.

QUINCE Marry, our play is 'The most lamentable comedy and most cruel death of Pyramus and Thisbe.'

BOTTOM A very good piece of work, I assure you, and a merry. Now, good Peter Quince, call forth your actors by the scroll. Masters, spread yourselves.

QUINCE Answer as I call you. Nick Bottom, the weaver.

BOTTOM Ready. Name what part I am for, and proceed.

QUINCE You, Nick Bottom, are set down for Pyramus.

BOTTOM What is Pyramus, a lover or a tyrant?

QUINCE A lover that kills himself most gallantly for love.

BOTTOM That will ask some tears in the true performing of it. If I do it, let the audience look to their eyes: I will move storms; I will condole in some measure. To the rest — yet my chief humour is for a tyrant: I could play Ercles rarely, or a part to tear a cat in, to make all split.

> The raging rocks
> And shivering shocks
> Shall break the locks
> Of prison gates.

> And Phibbus' car
> Shall shine from far
> And make and mar
> The foolish Fates.

This was lofty. Now name the rest of the players. This is Ercles' vein, a tyrant's vein: a lover is more condoling.

QUINCE Francis Flute, the bellows-mender.

FLUTE Here, Peter Quince.

QUINCE You must take Thisbe on you.

FLUTE What is Thisbe? A wand'ring knight?

QUINCE It is the lady that Pyramus must love.

FLUTE Nay, faith, let not me play a woman: I have a beard coming.

QUINCE That's all one. You shall play it in a mask, and you may speak as small as you will.

BOTTOM An I may hide my face, let me play Thisbe too. I'll speak in a monstrous little voice. 'Thisne, Thisne!' 'Ah, Pyramus, my lover dear! Thy Thisbe dear and lady dear!'

QUINCE No, no, you must play Pyramus.— And, Flute, you Thisbe.

BOTTOM Well, proceed.

QUINCE Robin Starveling, the tailor.

STARVELING Here, Peter Quince.

QUINCE Robin Starveling, you must play Thisbe's mother. Tom Snout, the tinker.

SNOUT Here, Peter Quince.

QUINCE You, Pyramus' father; myself, Thisbe's father;
Snug the joiner, you, the lion's part: and I hope there
is a play fitted.

SNUG Have you the lion's part written? Pray you, if it be,
give it me, for I am slow of study.

QUINCE You may do it extempore, for it is nothing but
roaring.

BOTTOM Let me play the lion too: I will roar that I will do
any man's heart good to hear me. I will roar that I
will make the duke say 'Let him roar again, let him
roar again.'

QUINCE If you should do it too terribly, you would fright
the duchess and the ladies that they would shriek,
and that were enough to hang us all.

ALL That would hang us, every mother's son.

BOTTOM I grant you, friends, if that you should fright the
ladies out of their wits, they would have no more
discretion but to hang us: but I will aggravate my
voice so that I will roar you as gently as any sucking
dove. I will roar an 'twere any nightingale.

QUINCE You can play no part but Pyramus, for Pyramus
is a sweet-faced man, a proper man, as one shall see
in a summer's day; a most lovely gentlemanlike man:
therefore you must needs play Pyramus.

BOTTOM Well, I will undertake it. What beard were I
best to play it in?

QUINCE Why, what you will.

BOTTOM I will discharge it in either your straw-colour beard, your orange-tawny beard, your purple-in-grain beard, or your French-crown-coloured beard, your perfect yellow.

QUINCE Some of your French crowns have no hair at all, and then you will play bare-faced. But, masters, here are your parts: and I am to entreat you, request you and desire you, to con them by tomorrow night, and meet me in the palace wood a mile without the town by moonlight. There will we rehearse, for if we meet in the city we shall be dogged with company, and our devices known. In the meantime I will draw a bill of properties, such as our play wants. I pray you fail me not.

BOTTOM We will meet, and there we may rehearse more obscenely and courageously. Take pains, be perfect. Adieu.

QUINCE At the duke's oak we meet.

BOTTOM Enough. Hold or cut bow-strings.   *Exeunt*

Act 2 [Scene 1]   *running scene 3*

Enter a Fairy at one door and Robin Goodfellow [Puck] at another

ROBIN How now, spirit, whither wander you?

FAIRY   Over hill, over dale,
             Through bush, through brier,

    Over park, over pale,
    Thorough flood, thorough fire,
    I do wander everywhere,
    Swifter than the moon's sphere;
    And I serve the fairy queen,
    To dew her orbs upon the green.
    The cowslips tall her pensioners be,
    In their gold coats spots you see,
    Those be rubies, fairy favours,
    In those freckles live their savours.
    I must go seek some dewdrops here,
    And hang a pearl in every cowslip's ear.
Farewell, thou lob of spirits, I'll be gone:
Our queen and all her elves come here anon.
ROBIN The king doth keep his revels here tonight:
Take heed the queen come not within his sight,
For Oberon is passing fell and wrath,
Because that she as her attendant hath
A lovely boy, stol'n from an Indian king.
She never had so sweet a changeling,
And jealous Oberon would have the child
Knight of his train, to trace the forests wild.
But she perforce withholds the lovèd boy,
Crowns him with flowers and makes him all her joy.
And now they never meet in grove or green,
By fountain clear or spangled starlight sheen,
But they do square, that all their elves for fear
Creep into acorn cups and hide them there.

FAIRY Either I mistake your shape and making quite,
    Or else you are that shrewd and knavish sprite
    Called Robin Goodfellow. Are not you he
    That frights the maidens of the villagery,
    Skim milk, and sometimes labour in the quern,
    And bootless make the breathless housewife churn,
    And sometime make the drink to bear no barm,
    Mislead night-wanderers, laughing at their harm?
    Those that Hobgoblin call you and sweet Puck,
    You do their work and they shall have good luck.
    Are not you he?
ROBIN Thou speak'st aright;
    I am that merry wanderer of the night.
    I jest to Oberon and make him smile
    When I a fat and bean-fed horse beguile,
    Neighing in likeness of a filly foal,
    And sometime lurk I in a gossip's bowl,
    In very likeness of a roasted crab,
    And when she drinks, against her lips I bob
    And on her withered dewlap pour the ale.
    The wisest aunt, telling the saddest tale,
    Sometime for three-foot stool mistaketh me,
    Then slip I from her bum, down topples she,
    And 'tailor' cries, and falls into a cough.
    And then the whole quire hold their hips and laugh,
    And waxen in their mirth and neeze and swear
    A merrier hour was never wasted there.
    But, room, fairy! Here comes Oberon.

FAIRY And here my mistress. Would that he were gone!
Enter the King of Fairies [Oberon] at one door with his train,
and the Queen [Titania] at another with hers

OBERON Ill met by moonlight, proud Titania.

TITANIA What, jealous Oberon? Fairies, skip hence.
    I have forsworn his bed and company.

OBERON Tarry, rash wanton, am not I thy lord?

TITANIA Then I must be thy lady: but I know
    When thou hast stol'n away from fairy land,
    And in the shape of Corin sat all day,
    Playing on pipes of corn and versing love
    To amorous Phillida. Why art thou here,
    Come from the farthest step of India?
    But that, forsooth, the bouncing Amazon,
    Your buskined mistress and your warrior love,
    To Theseus must be wedded; and you come
    To give their bed joy and prosperity?

OBERON How canst thou thus for shame, Titania,
    Glance at my credit with Hippolyta,
    Knowing I know thy love to Theseus?
    Didst not thou lead him through the glimmering night
    From Perigenia whom he ravishèd?
    And make him with fair Aegles break his faith,
    With Ariadne and Antiopa?

TITANIA These are the forgeries of jealousy,
    And never since the middle summer's spring
    Met we on hill, in dale, forest or mead,
    By pavèd fountain or by rushy brook,

Or in the beachèd margent of the sea,
To dance our ringlets to the whistling wind,
But with thy brawls thou hast disturbed our sport.
Therefore the winds, piping to us in vain,
As in revenge, have sucked up from the sea
Contagious fogs, which falling in the land
Hath every petty river made so proud
That they have overborne their continents.
The ox hath therefore stretched his yoke in vain,
The ploughman lost his sweat, and the green corn
Hath rotted ere his youth attained a beard.
The fold stands empty in the drownèd field,
And crows are fatted with the murrion flock,
The nine men's morris is filled up with mud,
And the quaint mazes in the wanton green
For lack of tread are undistinguishable.
The human mortals want their winter here:
No night is now with hymn or carol blessed.
Therefore the moon, the governess of floods,
Pale in her anger, washes all the air,
That rheumatic diseases do abound.
And through this distemperature we see
The seasons alter; hoary-headed frosts
Fall in the fresh lap of the crimson rose,
And on old Hiems' thin and icy crown
An odorous chaplet of sweet summer buds
Is, as in mockery, set. The spring, the summer,
The childing autumn, angry winter, change

Their wonted liveries, and the mazèd world
By their increase now knows not which is which;
And this same progeny of evils comes
From our debate, from our dissension:
We are their parents and original.

OBERON Do you amend it then, it lies in you.
Why should Titania cross her Oberon?
I do but beg a little changeling boy
To be my henchman.

TITANIA Set your heart at rest:
The fairy land buys not the child of me.
His mother was a votress of my order,
And in the spicèd Indian air by night
Full often hath she gossiped by my side,
And sat with me on Neptune's yellow sands,
Marking th'embarkèd traders on the flood,
When we have laughed to see the sails conceive
And grow big-bellied with the wanton wind,
Which she, with pretty and with swimming gait
Following — her womb then rich with my young
    squire —
Would imitate, and sail upon the land,
To fetch me trifles, and return again
As from a voyage, rich with merchandise.
But she, being mortal, of that boy did die:
And for her sake do I rear up her boy,
And for her sake I will not part with him.

OBERON How long within this wood intend you stay?

TITANIA Perchance till after Theseus' wedding day.
    If you will patiently dance in our round
    And see our moonlight revels, go with us;
    If not, shun me, and I will spare your haunts.

OBERON Give me that boy, and I will go with thee.

TITANIA Not for thy fairy kingdom. Fairies, away.
    We shall chide downright, if I longer stay.

                    Exeunt [Titania and her train]

OBERON Well, go thy way: thou shalt not from this grove
    Till I torment thee for this injury.
    My gentle Puck, come hither. Thou rememb'rest
    Since once I sat upon a promontory,
    And heard a mermaid on a dolphin's back
    Uttering such dulcet and harmonious breath
    That the rude sea grew civil at her song,
    And certain stars shot madly from their spheres
    To hear the sea-maid's music.

ROBIN I remember.

OBERON That very time I saw, but thou couldst not,
    Flying between the cold moon and the earth,
    Cupid all armed; a certain aim he took
    At a fair vestal thronèd by the west,
    And loosed his love-shaft smartly from his bow,
    As it should pierce a hundred thousand hearts.
    But I might see young Cupid's fiery shaft
    Quenched in the chaste beams of the wat'ry moon;
    And the imperial votress passèd on,
    In maiden meditation, fancy-free.

Yet marked I where the bolt of Cupid fell.
It fell upon a little western flower,
Before milk-white, now purple with love's wound,
And maidens call it love-in-idleness.
Fetch me that flower; the herb I showed thee once:
The juice of it on sleeping eyelids laid
Will make or man or woman madly dote
Upon the next live creature that it sees.
Fetch me this herb, and be thou here again
Ere the leviathan can swim a league.

ROBIN I'll put a girdle round about the earth
In forty minutes.   [*Exit*]

OBERON Having once this juice,
I'll watch Titania when she is asleep,
And drop the liquor of it in her eyes.
The next thing when she waking looks upon,
Be it on lion, bear, or wolf or bull,
On meddling monkey or on busy ape,
She shall pursue it with the soul of love.
And ere I take this charm off from her sight,
As I can take it with another herb,
I'll make her render up her page to me.
But who comes here? I am invisible,
And I will overhear their conference.

Enter Demetrius, Helena following him

DEMETRIUS I love thee not, therefore pursue me not.
Where is Lysander and fair Hermia?
The one I'll stay, the other stayeth me.

Thou told'st me they were stolen into this wood;
And here am I, and wood within this wood,
Because I cannot meet my Hermia.
Hence, get thee gone, and follow me no more.

HELENA You draw me, you hard-hearted adamant;
But yet you draw not iron, for my heart
Is true as steel. Leave you your power to draw,
And I shall have no power to follow you.

DEMETRIUS Do I entice you? Do I speak you fair?
Or rather do I not in plainest truth
Tell you I do not nor I cannot love you?

HELENA And even for that do I love thee the more.
I am your spaniel, and, Demetrius,
The more you beat me, I will fawn on you.
Use me but as your spaniel: spurn me, strike me,
Neglect me, lose me; only give me leave,
Unworthy as I am, to follow you.
What worser place can I beg in your love —
And yet a place of high respect with me —
Than to be used as you do use your dog?

DEMETRIUS Tempt not too much the hatred of my spirit,
For I am sick when I do look on thee.

HELENA And I am sick when I look not on you.

DEMETRIUS You do impeach your modesty too much,
To leave the city and commit yourself
Into the hands of one that loves you not,
To trust the opportunity of night

And the ill counsel of a desert place
With the rich worth of your virginity.

HELENA Your virtue is my privilege: for that
It is not night when I do see your face,
Therefore I think I am not in the night.
Nor doth this wood lack worlds of company,
For you in my respect are all the world.
Then how can it be said I am alone,
When all the world is here to look on me?

DEMETRIUS I'll run from thee and hide me in the brakes,
And leave thee to the mercy of wild beasts.

HELENA The wildest hath not such a heart as you.
Run when you will, the story shall be changed:
Apollo flies, and Daphne holds the chase;
The dove pursues the griffin, the mild hind
Makes speed to catch the tiger. Bootless speed,
When cowardice pursues and valour flies.

DEMETRIUS I will not stay thy questions, let me go;
Or if thou follow me, do not believe
But I shall do thee mischief in the wood.

[*Exit Demetrius*]

HELENA Ay, in the temple, in the town, the field,
You do me mischief. Fie, Demetrius!
Your wrongs do set a scandal on my sex:
We cannot fight for love, as men may do;
We should be wooed and were not made to woo.
I'll follow thee and make a heaven of hell,
To die upon the hand I love so well.   *Exit*

OBERON Fare thee well, nymph: ere he do leave this grove,
  Thou shalt fly him and he shall seek thy love.
Enter [Robin] Puck
  Hast thou the flower there? Welcome, wanderer.
ROBIN Ay, there it is.
OBERON I pray thee give it me.
  I know a bank where the wild thyme blows,
  Where oxlips and the nodding violet grows,
  Quite over-canopied with luscious woodbine,
  With sweet musk-roses and with eglantine:
  There sleeps Titania sometime of the night,
  Lulled in these flowers with dances and delight:
  And there the snake throws her enamelled skin,
  Weed wide enough to wrap a fairy in.
  And with the juice of this I'll streak her eyes,
  And make her full of hateful fantasies.
  Take thou some of it, and seek through this grove;
  A sweet Athenian lady is in love
  With a disdainful youth: anoint his eyes,
  But do it when the next thing he espies
  May be the lady. Thou shalt know the man
  By the Athenian garments he hath on.
  Effect it with some care, that he may prove
  More fond on her than she upon her love;
  And look thou meet me ere the first cock crow.
ROBIN Fear not, my lord, your servant shall do so.
                                                    Exeunt

[Act 2 Scene 2]   *running scene 4*

Enter Queen of Fairies [Titania] with her train

TITANIA Come, now a roundel and a fairy song;
　　Then, for the third part of a minute, hence:
　　Some to kill cankers in the musk-rose buds,
　　Some war with reremice for their leathern wings,
　　To make my small elves coats, and some keep back
　　The clamorous owl that nightly hoots and wonders
　　At our quaint spirits. Sing me now asleep,
　　Then to your offices and let me rest.
Fairies sing
FIRST FAIRY You spotted snakes with double tongue,
　　　　　　Thorny hedgehogs, be not seen.
　　　　　　Newts and blind-worms, do no wrong,
　　　　　　Come not near our fairy queen.
CHORUS　　Philomel, with melody
　　　　　　Sing in our sweet lullaby,
　　　　　　Lulla, lulla, lullaby, lulla, lulla, lullaby.
　　　　　　Never harm,
　　　　　　Nor spell nor charm,
　　　　　　Come our lovely lady nigh;
　　　　　　So, goodnight, with lullaby.
SECOND FAIRY Weaving spiders, come not here.
　　　　　　Hence, you long-legged spinners, hence!
　　　　　　Beetles black, approach not near;
　　　　　　Worm nor snail, do no offence.

CHORUS   Philomel, with melody, etc.
FIRST FAIRY Hence, away! Now all is well;
            One aloof stand sentinel.

                    She [Titania] sleeps. [Exeunt Fairies]

Enter Oberon

OBERON What thou see'st when thou dost wake,
      Do it for thy true-love take,
      Love and languish for his sake.
      Be it ounce or cat or bear,
      Pard, or boar with bristled hair,
      In thy eye that shall appear
      When thou wak'st, it is thy dear.
      Wake when some vile thing is near.   *[Exit]*

Enter Lysander and Hermia

LYSANDER Fair love, you faint with wand'ring in the wood,
      And to speak troth, I have forgot our way:
      We'll rest us, Hermia, if you think it good,
      And tarry for the comfort of the day.

HERMIA Be it so, Lysander; find you out a bed,
      For I upon this bank will rest my head.

LYSANDER One turf shall serve as pillow for us both:
      One heart, one bed, two bosoms and one troth.

HERMIA Nay, good Lysander, for my sake, my dear,
      Lie further off yet, do not lie so near.

LYSANDER O, take the sense, sweet, of my innocence!
      Love takes the meaning in love's conference.
      I mean that my heart unto yours is knit

So that but one heart we can make of it.
Two bosoms interchainèd with an oath,
So then two bosoms and a single troth.
Then by your side no bed-room me deny,
For lying so, Hermia, I do not lie.

HERMIA Lysander riddles very prettily.
Now much beshrew my manners and my pride,
If Hermia meant to say Lysander lied.
But, gentle friend, for love and courtesy
Lie further off, in human modesty:
Such separation as may well be said
Becomes a virtuous bachelor and a maid,
So far be distant, and good night, sweet friend;
Thy love ne'er alter till thy sweet life end!

LYSANDER Amen, amen, to that fair prayer, say I,
And then end life when I end loyalty!
Here is my bed: sleep give thee all his rest!

HERMIA With half that wish the wisher's eyes be pressed!

They sleep

Enter [Robin] Puck

ROBIN Through the forest have I gone,
But Athenian found I none
On whose eyes I might approve
This flower's force in stirring love.
Night and silence — who is here?
Weeds of Athens he doth wear:
This is he, my master said,

Despisèd the Athenian maid:
And here the maiden, sleeping sound,
On the dank and dirty ground.
Pretty soul, she durst not lie
Near this lack-love, this kill-courtesy.
Churl, upon thy eyes I throw
All the power this charm doth owe.
When thou wak'st, let love forbid
Sleep his seat on thy eyelid.
So awake when I am gone,
For I must now to Oberon.   *Exit*

Enter Demetrius and Helena, running

HELENA Stay, though thou kill me, sweet Demetrius.

DEMETRIUS I charge thee, hence, and do not haunt
      me thus.

HELENA O, wilt thou darkling leave me? Do not so.

DEMETRIUS Stay, on thy peril: I alone will go.   *Exit*

HELENA O, I am out of breath in this fond chase!
      The more my prayer, the lesser is my grace.
      Happy is Hermia, wheresoe'er she lies;
      For she hath blessèd and attractive eyes.
      How came her eyes so bright? Not with salt tears:
      If so, my eyes are oftener washed than hers.
      No, no, I am as ugly as a bear;
      For beasts that meet me run away for fear:
      Therefore no marvel though Demetrius
      Do, as a monster, fly my presence thus.
      What wicked and dissembling glass of mine

Made me compare with Hermia's sphery eyne?
But who is here? Lysander, on the ground;
Dead, or asleep? I see no blood, no wound.
Lysander if you live, good sir, awake.

LYSANDER And run through fire I will for thy sweet sake.
Transparent Helena, nature shows her art
That through thy bosom makes me see thy heart.
Where is Demetrius? O, how fit a word
Is that vile name to perish on my sword!

HELENA Do not say so, Lysander, say not so.
What though he love your Hermia? Lord, what
    though?
Yet Hermia still loves you; then be content.

LYSANDER Content with Hermia? No, I do repent
The tedious minutes I with her have spent.
Not Hermia but Helena now I love;
Who will not change a raven for a dove?
The will of man is by his reason swayed,
And reason says you are the worthier maid.
Things growing are not ripe until their season;
So I, being young, till now ripe not to reason.
And touching now the point of human skill,
Reason becomes the marshal to my will
And leads me to your eyes, where I o'erlook
Love's stories written in love's richest book.

HELENA Wherefore was I to this keen mockery born?
When at your hands did I deserve this scorn?
Is't not enough, is't not enough, young man,

That I did never, no, nor never can,
Deserve a sweet look from Demetrius' eye,
But you must flout my insufficiency?
Good troth you do me wrong, good sooth, you do,
In such disdainful manner me to woo.
But fare you well; perforce I must confess
I thought you lord of more true gentleness.
O, that a lady of one man refused
Should of another therefore be abused!   *Exit*

LYSANDER She sees not Hermia. Hermia, sleep thou there,
And never mayst thou come Lysander near;
For as a surfeit of the sweetest things
The deepest loathing to the stomach brings,
Or as the heresies that men do leave
Are hated most of those they did deceive,
So thou, my surfeit and my heresy,
Of all be hated, but the most of me.
And all my powers address your love and might
To honour Helen and to be her knight!   *Exit*

HERMIA Help me, Lysander, help me; do thy best
To pluck this crawling serpent from my breast!
Ay me, for pity; what a dream was here?
Lysander, look how I do quake with fear:
Methought a serpent ate my heart away,
And you sat smiling at his cruel prey.
Lysander! What, removed? Lysander! Lord!
What, out of hearing? Gone? No sound, no word?

Alack, where are you? Speak, an if you hear:
Speak, of all loves! I swoon almost with fear.
No? Then I well perceive you are not nigh.
Either death or you I'll find immediately.

Exit

Act 3 [Scene 1]   *running scene 4 continues*

Enter the Clowns [Bottom, Quince, Snug, Flute, Snout and Starveling]

BOTTOM Are we all met?

QUINCE Pat, pat, and here's a marvellous convenient place for our rehearsal. This green plot shall be our stage, this hawthorn brake our tiring-house, and we will do it in action as we will do it before the duke.

BOTTOM Peter Quince?

QUINCE What sayest thou, bully Bottom?

BOTTOM There are things in this comedy of Pyramus and Thisbe that will never please. First, Pyramus must draw a sword to kill himself; which the ladies cannot abide. How answer you that?

SNOUT By'r lakin, a parlous fear.

STARVELING I believe we must leave the killing out, when all is done.

BOTTOM Not a whit: I have a device to make all well. Write me a prologue, and let the prologue seem to say we will do no harm with our swords, and that

Pyramus is not killed indeed. And for the more better assurance, tell them that I, Pyramus, am not Pyramus, but Bottom the weaver; this will put them out of fear.

QUINCE Well, we will have such a prologue, and it shall be written in eight and six.

BOTTOM No, make it two more: let it be written in eight and eight.

SNOUT Will not the ladies be afeard of the lion?

STARVELING I fear it, I promise you.

BOTTOM Masters, you ought to consider with yourselves, to bring in — God shield us! — a lion among ladies is a most dreadful thing. For there is not a more fearful wild-fowl than your lion living. And we ought to look to it.

SNOUT Therefore another prologue must tell he is not a lion.

BOTTOM Nay, you must name his name, and half his face must be seen through the lion's neck, and he himself must speak through, saying thus, or to the same defect: 'Ladies' or 'Fair-ladies, I would wish you' or 'I would request you' or 'I would entreat you, not to fear, not to tremble. My life for yours. If you think I come hither as a lion, it were pity of my life. No, I am no such thing, I am a man as other men are.' And there indeed let him name his name, and tell them plainly he is Snug the joiner.

QUINCE Well, it shall be so. But there is two hard things:
that is, to bring the moonlight into a chamber, for
you know Pyramus and Thisbe meet by moonlight.

SNOUT Doth the moon shine that night we play our
play?

BOTTOM A calendar, a calendar! Look in the almanac.
Find out moonshine, find out moonshine.

[*Robin may*] *enter*

QUINCE Yes, it doth shine that night.

BOTTOM Why, then may you leave a casement of the
great chamber window, where we play, open, and
the moon may shine in at the casement.

QUINCE Ay, or else one must come in with a bush of
thorns and a lantern, and say he comes to disfigure,
or to present, the person of Moonshine. Then there is
another thing: we must have a wall in the great
chamber; for Pyramus and Thisbe, says the story, did
talk through the chink of a wall.

SNOUT You can never bring in a wall. What say you,
Bottom?

BOTTOM Some man or other must present Wall: and let
him have some plaster, or some loam, or some
rough-cast about him, to signify wall; or let him hold
his fingers thus; and through that cranny shall
Pyramus and Thisbe whisper.

QUINCE If that may be, then all is well. Come, sit down,
every mother's son, and rehearse your parts.
Pyramus, you begin: when you have spoken your

speech, enter into that brake, and so every one according to his cue.

Robin [may] enter

ROBIN What hempen home-spuns have we swagg'ring here,

So near the cradle of the fairy queen?

What, a play toward? I'll be an auditor,

An actor too perhaps, if I see cause.

QUINCE Speak, Pyramus.— Thisbe, stand forth.

PYRAMUS [BOTTOM] Thisbe, the flowers of odious savours sweet—

QUINCE Odours, odours.

PYRAMUS [BOTTOM] —odours savours sweet,

So hath thy breath, my dearest Thisbe dear.

But hark, a voice! Stay thou but here awhile,

And by and by I will to thee appear.   *Exit*

ROBIN A stranger Pyramus than e'er played here. [*Exit*]

THISBE [FLUTE] Must I speak now?

QUINCE Ay, marry, must you, for you must understand he goes but to see a noise that he heard, and is to come again.

THISBE [FLUTE] Most radiant Pyramus, most lily-white of hue,

Of colour like the red rose on triumphant brier,

Most brisky juvenal and eke most lovely Jew,

As true as truest horse that yet would never tire,

I'll meet thee, Pyramus, at Ninny's tomb.

QUINCE 'Ninus' tomb', man! Why, you must not speak
that yet; that you answer to Pyramus. You speak all
your part at once, cues and all. Pyramus, enter: your
cue is past; it is, 'never tire'.

THISBE [FLUTE] O — As true as truest horse that yet
would never tire.

Enter [Robin and] Pyramus [Bottom] with the ass head

PYRAMUS [BOTTOM] If I were fair, Thisbe, I were only
thine.

QUINCE O monstrous! O strange! We are haunted. Pray,
masters! Fly, masters! Help!   *The Clowns all exit*

ROBIN I'll follow you, I'll lead you about a round,
Through bog, through bush, through brake, through
brier.
Sometime a horse I'll be, sometime a hound,
A hog, a headless bear, sometime a fire,
And neigh and bark and grunt and roar and burn,
Like horse, hound, hog, bear, fire, at every
turn.   *Exit*

BOTTOM Why do they run away? This is a knavery of
them to make me afeard.

Enter Snout

SNOUT O Bottom, thou art changed! What do I see on
thee?

BOTTOM What do you see? You see an asshead of your
own, do you?   *[Exit Snout]*

Enter Quince

QUINCE Bless thee, Bottom! Bless thee! Thou art
translated.   *Exit*

BOTTOM I see their knavery: this is to make an ass of me,
to fright me, if they could; but I will not stir from this
place, do what they can. I will walk up and down here,
and I will sing, that they shall hear I am not afraid.

> The ousel cock so black of hue,
> With orange-tawny bill,
> The throstle with his note so true,
> The wren with little quill—

TITANIA What angel wakes me from my flow'ry bed?

BOTTOM The finch, the sparrow and the lark,

> The plain-song cuckoo grey,
> Whose note full many a man doth mark,
> And dares not answer nay —

For, indeed, who would set his wit to so foolish a
bird? Who would give a bird the lie, though he cry
'cuckoo' never so?

TITANIA I pray thee, gentle mortal, sing again:
Mine ear is much enamoured of thy note;
So is mine eye enthrallèd to thy shape:
And thy fair virtue's force perforce doth move me
On the first view to say, to swear, I love thee.

BOTTOM Methinks, mistress, you should have little
reason for that: and yet, to say the truth, reason
and love keep little company together nowadays; the
more the pity that some honest neighbours will not
make them friends. Nay, I can gleek upon occasion.

TITANIA Thou art as wise as thou art beautiful.

BOTTOM Not so, neither: but if I had wit enough to get out of this wood, I have enough to serve mine own turn.

TITANIA Out of this wood do not desire to go:
Thou shalt remain here, whether thou wilt or no.
I am a spirit of no common rate.
The summer still doth tend upon my state,
And I do love thee: therefore, go with me.
I'll give thee fairies to attend on thee,
And they shall fetch thee jewels from the deep,
And sing while thou on pressèd flowers dost sleep.
And I will purge thy mortal grossness so
That thou shalt like an airy spirit go.
Peaseblossom, Cobweb, Moth, Mustardseed!

Enter four Fairies

PEASEBLOSSOM Ready.

COBWEB And I.

MOTH And I.

MUSTARDSEED And I.

ALL Where shall we go?

TITANIA Be kind and courteous to this gentleman.
Hop in his walks and gambol in his eyes,
Feed him with apricocks and dewberries,
With purple grapes, green figs, and mulberries.
The honey-bags steal from the humble-bees,
And for night-tapers crop their waxen thighs
And light them at the fiery glow-worm's eyes,

To have my love to bed and to arise.
And pluck the wings from painted butterflies
To fan the moonbeams from his sleeping eyes.
Nod to him, elves, and do him courtesies.

PEASEBLOSSOM Hail, mortal!

COBWEB Hail!

MOTH Hail!

MUSTARDSEED Hail!

BOTTOM I cry your worship's mercy, heartily; I beseech
your worship's name.

COBWEB Cobweb.

BOTTOM I shall desire you of more acquaintance, good
Master Cobweb: if I cut my finger, I shall make bold
with you.— Your name, honest gentleman?

PEASEBLOSSOM Peaseblossom.

BOTTOM I pray you commend me to Mistress Squash,
your mother, and to Master Peascod, your father.
Good Master Peaseblossom, I shall desire you of more
acquaintance too.— Your name, I beseech you, sir?

MUSTARDSEED Mustardseed.

BOTTOM Good Master Mustardseed, I know your
patience well: that same cowardly, giant-like ox-
beef hath devoured many a gentleman of your house.
I promise you, your kindred hath made my eyes
water ere now. I desire you of more acquaintance,
good Master Mustardseed.

TITANIA Come, wait upon him, lead him to my bower.
The moon methinks looks with a wat'ry eye,

And when she weeps, weeps every little flower,
Lamenting some enforcèd chastity.
Tie up my lover's tongue, bring him silently. *Exeunt*

[Act 3 Scene 2]   *running scene 5*

Enter King of Fairies [Oberon] alone

OBERON I wonder if Titania be awaked;
  Then what it was that next came in her eye,
  Which she must dote on in extremity.
Enter [Robin] Puck
  Here comes my messenger.— How now, mad spirit?
  What night-rule now about this haunted grove?
ROBIN My mistress with a monster is in love.
  Near to her close and consecrated bower,
  While she was in her dull and sleeping hour,
  A crew of patches, rude mechanicals,
  That work for bread upon Athenian stalls,
  Were met together to rehearse a play
  Intended for great Theseus' nuptial-day.
  The shallowest thick-skin of that barren sort,
  Who Pyramus presented in their sport,
  Forsook his scene and entered in a brake,
  When I did him at this advantage take:
  An ass's noll I fixèd on his head.
  Anon his Thisbe must be answerèd,
  And forth my mimic comes. When they him spy,

As wild geese that the creeping fowler eye,
Or russet-pated choughs, many in sort,
Rising and cawing at the gun's report,
Sever themselves and madly sweep the sky,
So, at his sight, away his fellows fly.
And at our stamp here o'er and o'er one falls;
He 'murder' cries and help from Athens calls.
Their sense thus weak, lost with their fears thus strong,
Made senseless things begin to do them wrong.
For briars and thorns at their apparel snatch,
Some sleeves, some hats, from yielders all things catch.
I led them on in this distracted fear,
And left sweet Pyramus translated there:
When in that moment, so it came to pass,
Titania waked and straightway loved an ass.

OBERON This falls out better than I could devise.
But hast thou yet latched the Athenian's eyes
With the love juice, as I did bid thee do?

ROBIN I took him sleeping — that is finished too —
And the Athenian woman by his side,
That, when he waked, of force she must be eyed.

Enter Demetrius and Hermia

OBERON Stand close. This is the same Athenian.

ROBIN This is the woman, but not this the man.

DEMETRIUS O, why rebuke you him that loves you so?
Lay breath so bitter on your bitter foe.

HERMIA Now I but chide, but I should use thee worse,
For thou, I fear, hast given me cause to curse,

If thou hast slain Lysander in his sleep,
Being o'er shoes in blood, plunge in the deep,
And kill me too.
The sun was not so true unto the day
As he to me. Would he have stol'n away
From sleeping Hermia? I'll believe as soon
This whole earth may be bored and that the moon
May through the centre creep, and so displease
Her brother's noontide with th'Antipodes.
It cannot be but thou hast murdered him,
So should a murderer look, so dead, so grim.

DEMETRIUS So should the murdered look, and so should I,
Pierced through the heart with your stern cruelty:
Yet you, the murderer, looks as bright, as clear,
As yonder Venus in her glimm'ring sphere.

HERMIA What's this to my Lysander? Where is he?
Ah, good Demetrius, wilt thou give him me?

DEMETRIUS I'd rather give his carcass to my hounds.

HERMIA Out, dog! Out, cur! Thou driv'st me past the bounds
Of maiden's patience. Hast thou slain him, then?
Henceforth be never numbered among men.
O, once tell true, tell true even for my sake!
Durst thou a looked upon him being awake?
And hast thou killed him sleeping? O brave touch!
Could not a worm, an adder, do so much?
An adder did it, for with doubler tongue
Than thine, thou serpent, never adder stung.

DEMETRIUS You spend your passion on a misprised mood.
  I am not guilty of Lysander's blood,
  Nor is he dead, for aught that I can tell.
HERMIA I pray thee tell me then that he is well.
DEMETRIUS An if I could, what should I get therefor?
HERMIA A privilege never to see me more;
  And from thy hated presence part I so:
  See me no more, whether he be dead or no.   *Exit*
DEMETRIUS There is no following her in this fierce vein:
  Here therefore for a while I will remain.
  So sorrow's heaviness doth heavier grow
  For debt that bankrupt sleep doth sorrow owe,
  Which now in some slight measure it will pay,
  If for his tender here I make some stay.

              [*Demetrius*] *lies down* [*and sleeps*]

OBERON What hast thou done? Thou hast mistaken quite
  And laid the love juice on some true love's sight:
  Of thy misprision must perforce ensue
  Some true love turned, and not a false turned true.
ROBIN Then fate o'errules, that, one man holding troth,
  A million fail, confounding oath on oath.
OBERON About the wood go swifter than the wind,
  And Helena of Athens look thou find.
  All fancy-sick she is and pale of cheer,
  With sighs of love, that costs the fresh blood dear.
  By some illusion see thou bring her here.
  I'll charm his eyes against she doth appear.

ROBIN I go, I go, look how I go,
  Swifter than arrow from the Tartar's bow.   *Exit*
OBERON Flower of this purple dye,
  Hit with Cupid's archery,
  Sink in apple of his eye.
  When his love he doth espy,
  Let her shine as glor'ously
  As the Venus of the sky.
  When thou wak'st, if she be by,
  Beg of her for remedy.
Enter [Robin] Puck
ROBIN Captain of our fairy band,
  Helena is here at hand,
  And the youth, mistook by me,
  Pleading for a lover's fee.
  Shall we their fond pageant see?
  Lord, what fools these mortals be!
OBERON Stand aside: the noise they make
  Will cause Demetrius to awake.
ROBIN Then will two at once woo one,
  That must needs be sport alone.
  And those things do best please me
  That befall preposterously.
Enter Lysander [following] Helena
LYSANDER Why should you think that I should woo in
    scorn?
  Scorn and derision never come in tears:
  Look when I vow, I weep; and vows so born,

In their nativity all truth appears.
How can these things in me seem scorn to you,
Bearing the badge of faith to prove them true?

HELENA You do advance your cunning more and more.
When truth kills truth, O devilish-holy fray!
These vows are Hermia's. Will you give her o'er?
Weigh oath with oath, and you will nothing weigh.
Your vows to her and me, put in two scales,
Will even weigh, and both as light as tales.

LYSANDER I had no judgement when to her I swore.

HELENA Nor none, in my mind, now you give her o'er.

LYSANDER Demetrius loves her, and he you.

DEMETRIUS O Helen, goddess, nymph, perfect, divine!

Awakes

To what, my love, shall I compare thine eyne?
Crystal is muddy. O, how ripe in show
Thy lips, those kissing cherries, tempting grow!
That pure congealèd white, high Taurus' snow,
Fanned with the eastern wind, turns to a crow
When thou hold'st up thy hand. O, let me kiss
This princess of pure white, this seal of bliss!

HELENA O spite! O hell! I see you all are bent
To set against me for your merriment:
If you were civil and knew courtesy,
You would not do me thus much injury.
Can you not hate me, as I know you do,
But you must join in souls to mock me too?
If you were men, as men you are in show,

You would not use a gentle lady so;
To vow, and swear, and superpraise my parts,
When I am sure you hate me with your hearts.
You both are rivals and love Hermia;
And now both rivals to mock Helena.
A trim exploit, a manly enterprise,
To conjure tears up in a poor maid's eyes
With your derision; none of noble sort
Would so offend a virgin and extort
A poor soul's patience, all to make you sport.

LYSANDER You are unkind, Demetrius; be not so,
For you love Hermia; this you know I know;
And here, with all good will, with all my heart,
In Hermia's love I yield you up my part;
And yours of Helena to me bequeath,
Whom I do love and will do till my death.

HELENA Never did mockers waste more idle breath.

DEMETRIUS Lysander, keep thy Hermia, I will none:
If e'er I loved her, all that love is gone.
My heart to her but as guestwise sojourned,
And now to Helen is it home returned,
There to remain.

LYSANDER Helen, it is not so.

DEMETRIUS Disparage not the faith thou dost not know,
Lest to thy peril thou abide it dear.
Look where thy love comes, yonder is thy dear.

Enter Hermia

HERMIA Dark night, that from the eye his function takes,
    The ear more quick of apprehension makes,
    Wherein it doth impair the seeing sense,
    It pays the hearing double recompense.
    Thou art not by mine eye, Lysander, found,
    Mine ear, I thank it, brought me to thy sound.
    But why unkindly didst thou leave me so?
LYSANDER Why should he stay whom love doth press
    to go?
HERMIA What love could press Lysander from my side?
LYSANDER Lysander's love, that would not let him bide —
    Fair Helena, who more engilds the night
    Than all yon fiery oes and eyes of light.—
    Why seek'st thou me? Could not this make thee know,
    The hate I bear thee made me leave thee so?
HERMIA You speak not as you think; it cannot be.
HELENA Lo, she is one of this confed'racy!
    Now I perceive they have conjoined all three
    To fashion this false sport in spite of me.
    Injurious Hermia, most ungrateful maid,
    Have you conspired, have you with these contrived
    To bait me with this foul derision?
    Is all the counsel that we two have shared,
    The sisters' vows, the hours that we have spent,
    When we have chid the hasty-footed time
    For parting us — O, is all forgot?
    All schooldays' friendship, childhood innocence?
    We, Hermia, like two artificial gods,

Have with our needles created both one flower,
Both on one sampler, sitting on one cushion,
Both warbling of one song, both in one key,
As if our hands, our sides, voices and minds,
Had been incorporate. So we grew together
Like to a double cherry, seeming parted,
But yet a union in partition,
Two lovely berries moulded on one stem,
So with two seeming bodies but one heart,
Two of the first, like coats in heraldry,
Due but to one and crownèd with one crest.
And will you rent our ancient love asunder,
To join with men in scorning your poor friend?
It is not friendly, 'tis not maidenly.
Our sex, as well as I, may chide you for it,
Though I alone do feel the injury.

HERMIA I am amazèd at your passionate words.
I scorn you not; it seems that you scorn me.

HELENA Have you not set Lysander, as in scorn,
To follow me and praise my eyes and face?
And made your other love, Demetrius,
Who even but now did spurn me with his foot,
To call me goddess, nymph, divine and rare,
Precious, celestial? Wherefore speaks he this
To her he hates? And wherefore doth Lysander
Deny your love, so rich within his soul,
And tender me, forsooth, affection,
But by your setting on, by your consent?

What though I be not so in grace as you,
So hung upon with love, so fortunate,
But miserable most, to love unloved?
This you should pity rather than despise.

HERMIA I understand not what you mean by this.

HELENA Ay, do. Persever, counterfeit sad looks,
Make mouths upon me when I turn my back,
Wink each at other, hold the sweet jest up:
This sport well carried shall be chronicled.
If you have any pity, grace, or manners,
You would not make me such an argument.
But fare ye well. 'Tis partly my own fault,
Which death or absence soon shall remedy.

LYSANDER Stay, gentle Helena, hear my excuse:
My love, my life, my soul, fair Helena!

HELENA O excellent!

HERMIA Sweet, do not scorn her so.

DEMETRIUS If she cannot entreat, I can compel.

LYSANDER Thou canst compel no more than she entreat.
Thy threats have no more strength than her weak
    prayers.
Helen, I love thee, by my life, I do;
I swear by that which I will lose for thee,
To prove him false that says I love thee not.

DEMETRIUS I say I love thee more than he can do.

LYSANDER If thou say so, withdraw, and prove it too.

DEMETRIUS Quick, come!

HERMIA Lysander, whereto tends all this?

LYSANDER Away, you Ethiope!

DEMETRIUS No, no, sir,
    Seem to break loose; take on as you would follow,
    But yet come not: you are a tame man, go!

LYSANDER Hang off, thou cat, thou burr! Vile thing, let
    loose,
    Or I will shake thee from me like a serpent!

HERMIA Why are you grown so rude?
    What change is this, sweet love?

LYSANDER Thy love? Out, tawny Tartar, out!
    Out, loathèd medicine! O hated potion, hence!

HERMIA Do you not jest?

HELENA Yes, sooth, and so do you.

LYSANDER Demetrius, I will keep my word with thee.

DEMETRIUS I would I had your bond, for I perceive
    A weak bond holds you; I'll not trust your word.

LYSANDER What, should I hurt her, strike her, kill her
    dead?
    Although I hate her, I'll not harm her so.

HERMIA What, can you do me greater harm than hate?
    Hate me? Wherefore? O me! What news, my love?
    Am not I Hermia? Are not you Lysander?
    I am as fair now as I was erewhile.
    Since night you loved me; yet since night you left me.
    Why, then you left me — O, the gods forbid! —
    In earnest, shall I say?

LYSANDER Ay, by my life;
    And never did desire to see thee more.

Therefore be out of hope, of question, of doubt;
Be certain, nothing truer: 'tis no jest
That I do hate thee and love Helena.

HERMIA O me! You juggler, you canker-blossom,
You thief of love! What, have you come by night
And stolen my love's heart from him?

HELENA Fine, i'faith!
Have you no modesty, no maiden shame,
No touch of bashfulness? What, will you tear
Impatient answers from my gentle tongue?
Fie, fie! You counterfeit, you puppet, you!

HERMIA Puppet? Why so? Ay, that way goes the game.
Now I perceive that she hath made compare
Between our statures, she hath urged her height,
And with her personage, her tall personage,
Her height, forsooth, she hath prevailed with him.
And are you grown so high in his esteem
Because I am so dwarfish and so low?
How low am I, thou painted maypole? Speak!
How low am I? I am not yet so low
But that my nails can reach unto thine eyes.

HELENA I pray you, though you mock me, gentlemen,
Let her not hurt me; I was never curst,
I have no gift at all in shrewishness;
I am a right maid for my cowardice;
Let her not strike me. You perhaps may think,
Because she is something lower than myself,
That I can match her.

HERMIA Lower? Hark, again.

HELENA Good Hermia, do not be so bitter with me.
  I evermore did love you, Hermia,
  Did ever keep your counsels, never wronged you,
  Save that, in love unto Demetrius,
  I told him of your stealth unto this wood.
  He followed you. For love I followed him.
  But he hath chid me hence and threatened me
  To strike me, spurn me, nay, to kill me too;
  And now, so you will let me quiet go,
  To Athens will I bear my folly back
  And follow you no further. Let me go.
  You see how simple and how fond I am.

HERMIA Why, get you gone: who is't that hinders you?

HELENA A foolish heart, that I leave here behind.

HERMIA What, with Lysander?

HELENA With Demetrius.

LYSANDER Be not afraid: she shall not harm thee, Helena.

DEMETRIUS No, sir, she shall not, though you take her part.

HELENA O, when she's angry, she is keen and shrewd.
  She was a vixen when she went to school,
  And though she be but little, she is fierce.

HERMIA 'Little' again! Nothing but 'low' and 'little'?
  Why will you suffer her to flout me thus?
  Let me come to her.

LYSANDER Get you gone, you dwarf,
  You minimus, of hind'ring knot-grass made!
  You bead, you acorn.

DEMETRIUS You are too officious
   In her behalf that scorns your services.
   Let her alone. Speak not of Helena,
   Take not her part. For if thou dost intend
   Never so little show of love to her,
   Thou shalt abide it.

LYSANDER Now she holds me not.
   Now follow, if thou dar'st, to try whose right,
   Of thine or mine, is most in Helena.

DEMETRIUS Follow? Nay, I'll go with thee, cheek by jowl.
                    Exeunt Lysander and Demetrius

HERMIA You, mistress, all this coil is 'long of you.
   Nay, go not back.

HELENA I will not trust you, I,
   Nor longer stay in your curst company.
   Your hands than mine are quicker for a fray,
   My legs are longer though, to run away.
              [*Exit Helena, running, followed by Hermia*]
Enter Oberon and [*Robin*] *Puck* [*coming forward*]

OBERON This is thy negligence. Still thou mistak'st,
   Or else committ'st thy knaveries wilfully.

ROBIN Believe me, king of shadows, I mistook.
   Did not you tell me I should know the man
   By the Athenian garments he hath on?
   And so far blameless proves my enterprise,
   That I have 'nointed an Athenian's eyes,
   And so far am I glad it so did sort,
   As this their jangling I esteem a sport.

OBERON Thou see'st these lovers seek a place to fight:
    Hie therefore, Robin, overcast the night,
    The starry welkin cover thou anon
    With drooping fog as black as Acheron,
    And lead these testy rivals so astray
    As one come not within another's way.
    Like to Lysander sometime frame thy tongue,
    Then stir Demetrius up with bitter wrong;
    And sometime rail thou like Demetrius;
    And from each other look thou lead them thus,
    Till o'er their brows death-counterfeiting sleep
    With leaden legs and batty wings doth creep;
    Then crush this herb into Lysander's eye,
    Whose liquor hath this virtuous property,
    To take from thence all error with his might,
    And make his eyeballs roll with wonted sight.
    When they next wake, all this derision
    Shall seem a dream and fruitless vision,
    And back to Athens shall the lovers wend
    With league whose date till death shall never end.
    Whiles I in this affair do thee employ,
    I'll to my queen and beg her Indian boy;
    And then I will her charmèd eye release
    From monster's view, and all things shall be peace.
ROBIN My fairy lord, this must be done with haste,
    For night-swift dragons cut the clouds full fast,
    And yonder shines Aurora's harbinger,

At whose approach, ghosts, wand'ring here and there,
Troop home to churchyards; damnèd spirits all,
That in crossways and floods have burial,
Already to their wormy beds are gone;
For fear lest day should look their shames upon,
They wilfully themselves exile from light
And must for aye consort with black-browed night.

OBERON But we are spirits of another sort:
I with the morning's love have oft made sport,
And, like a forester, the groves may tread,
Even till the eastern gate, all fiery red,
Opening on Neptune with fair blessèd beams,
Turns into yellow gold his salt green streams.
But notwithstanding, haste, make no delay:
We may effect this business yet ere day. *Exit*

ROBIN Up and down, up and down,
  I will lead them up and down.
  I am feared in field and town.
  Goblin, lead them up and down.
Here comes one.

Enter Lysander

LYSANDER Where art thou, proud Demetrius? Speak
  thou now.

ROBIN Here, villain, drawn and ready. Where art thou?

LYSANDER I will be with thee straight.

ROBIN Follow me, then, to plainer ground.

Enter Demetrius

DEMETRIUS Lysander, speak again;
    Thou runaway, thou coward, art thou fled?
    Speak! In some bush? Where dost thou hide thy head?
ROBIN Thou coward, art thou bragging to the stars,
    Telling the bushes that thou look'st for wars,
    And wilt not come? Come, recreant, come, thou child.
    I'll whip thee with a rod. He is defiled
    That draws a sword on thee.
DEMETRIUS Yea, art thou there?
ROBIN Follow my voice. We'll try no manhood here.

Exeunt

Enter Lysander
LYSANDER He goes before me and still dares me on.
    When I come where he calls, then he's gone.
    The villain is much lighter-heeled than I:
    I followed fast, but faster he did fly;
    That fallen am I in dark uneven way,
    And here will rest me. Come, thou gentle day!

Lie down

    For if but once thou show me thy grey light,
    I'll find Demetrius and revenge this spite.
Enter Robin and Demetrius, shifting places
ROBIN Ho, ho, ho! Coward, why com'st thou not?
DEMETRIUS Abide me, if thou dar'st, for well I wot
    Thou runn'st before me, shifting every place,
    And dar'st not stand, nor look me in the face.
    Where art thou now?
ROBIN Come hither. I am here.

DEMETRIUS Nay then, thou mock'st me. Thou shalt buy
    this dear
    If ever I thy face by daylight see.
    Now, go thy way: faintness constraineth me
    To measure out my length on this cold bed.
    By day's approach look to be visited.

Enter Helena

HELENA O weary night, O long and tedious night,
    Abate thy hours! Shine comforts from the east,
    That I may back to Athens by daylight,
    From these that my poor company detest;
    And sleep, that sometime shuts up sorrow's eye,
    Steal me awhile from mine own company.   *Sleep*

ROBIN Yet but three? Come one more,
    Two of both kinds make up four.
    Here she comes, curst and sad.
    Cupid is a knavish lad,

Enter Hermia

    Thus to make poor females mad.

HERMIA Never so weary, never so in woe,
    Bedabbled with the dew and torn with briers,
    I can no further crawl, no further go;
    My legs can keep no pace with my desires.
    Here will I rest me till the break of day.
    Heavens shield Lysander, if they mean a fray!

ROBIN On the ground
    Sleep sound.
    I'll apply

To your eye,
Gentle lover, remedy.
When thou wak'st,
Thou tak'st
True delight
In the sight
Of thy former lady's eye,
And the country proverb known,
That every man should take his own,
In your waking shall be shown.
Jack shall have Jill,
Naught shall go ill,
The man shall have his mare again, and all shall
    be well.   *Exit*

They [*Lysander, Demetrius,*
Helena and Hermia] *sleep all the act*

Act 4 [Scene 1]   *running scene 5 continues*

Enter Queen of Fairies [*Titania*] *and Clown* [*Bottom, with ass*
head, wearing a coronet of flowers] *and Fairies*
[*Peaseblossom, Cobweb, Moth, Mustardseed*] *and the King*
[*Oberon*] *behind them*

TITANIA Come, sit thee down upon this flow'ry bed,
    While I thy amiable cheeks do coy,
    And stick musk-roses in thy sleek smooth head,
    And kiss thy fair large ears, my gentle joy.

BOTTOM Where's Peaseblossom?

PEASEBLOSSOM Ready.

BOTTOM Scratch my head, Peaseblossom. Where's Monsieur Cobweb?

COBWEB Ready.

BOTTOM Monsieur Cobweb, good monsieur, get you your weapons in your hand, and kill me a red-hipped humble-bee on the top of a thistle; and, good monsieur, bring me the honey-bag. Do not fret yourself too much in the action, monsieur; and, good monsieur, have a care the honey-bag break not. I would be loath to have you overflown with a honey-bag, signior. Where's Monsieur Mustardseed?

MUSTARDSEED Ready.

BOTTOM Give me your neaf, Monsieur Mustardseed. Pray you leave your courtesy, good monsieur.

MUSTARDSEED What's your will?

BOTTOM Nothing, good monsieur, but to help Cavalery Cobweb to scratch. I must to the barber's, monsieur, for methinks I am marvellous hairy about the face. And I am such a tender ass, if my hair do but tickle me, I must scratch.

TITANIA What, wilt thou hear some music, my sweet love?

BOTTOM I have a reasonable good ear in music. Let us have the tongs and the bones.

Music: tongs, rural music

TITANIA Or say, sweet love, what thou desirest to eat.

BOTTOM Truly, a peck of provender; I could munch your
    good dry oats. Methinks I have a great desire to a
    bottle of hay: good hay, sweet hay, hath no fellow.

TITANIA I have a vent'rous fairy that shall seek
    The squirrel's hoard, and fetch thee new nuts.

BOTTOM I had rather have a handful or two of dried
    peas. But, I pray you let none of your people stir me. I
    have an exposition of sleep come upon me.

TITANIA Sleep thou, and I will wind thee in my arms.
    Fairies, begone, and be all ways away. [*Exeunt fairies*]
    So doth the woodbine the sweet honeysuckle
    Gently entwist; the female ivy so
    Enrings the barky fingers of the elm.
    O, how I love thee! How I dote on thee!

Enter Robin Goodfellow and Oberon [*who comes forward*]

OBERON Welcome, good Robin.
    See'st thou this sweet sight?
    Her dotage now I do begin to pity.
    For, meeting her of late behind the wood,
    Seeking sweet favours for this hateful fool,
    I did upbraid her and fall out with her.
    For she his hairy temples then had rounded
    With coronet of fresh and fragrant flowers.
    And that same dew, which sometime on the buds
    Was wont to swell like round and orient pearls,
    Stood now within the pretty flowerets' eyes
    Like tears that did their own disgrace bewail.
    When I had at my pleasure taunted her,

And she in mild terms begged my patience,
I then did ask of her her changeling child,
Which straight she gave me, and her fairy sent
To bear him to my bower in fairy land.
And now I have the boy, I will undo
This hateful imperfection of her eyes.
And, gentle Puck, take this transformèd scalp
From off the head of this Athenian swain;
That, he awaking when the other do,
May all to Athens back again repair,
And think no more of this night's accidents
But as the fierce vexation of a dream.
But first I will release the fairy queen.
Be thou as thou wast wont to be;
See as thou wast wont to see.
Dian's bud o'er Cupid's flower
Hath such force and blessèd power.
Now, my Titania, wake you, my sweet queen.

TITANIA My Oberon! What visions have I seen!
Methought I was enamoured of an ass.

OBERON There lies your love.

TITANIA How came these things to pass?
O, how mine eyes do loathe his visage now!

OBERON Silence awhile.— Robin, take off this head.—
Titania, music call, and strike more dead
Than common sleep of all these five the sense.

TITANIA Music, ho! Music, such as charmeth sleep!

Music, still

ROBIN Now, when thou wak'st, with thine own fool's
    eyes peep.
OBERON Sound, music! Come, my queen, take hands
    with me,
    And rock the ground whereon these sleepers be.
    Now thou and I are new in amity,
    And will tomorrow midnight solemnly
    Dance in Duke Theseus' house triumphantly,
    And bless it to all fair prosperity.
    There shall the pairs of faithful lovers be
    Wedded, with Theseus, all in jollity.
ROBIN Fairy king, attend, and mark:
    I do hear the morning lark.
OBERON Then, my queen, in silence sad,
    Trip we after the night's shade;
    We the globe can compass soon,
    Swifter than the wand'ring moon.
TITANIA Come, my lord, and in our flight
    Tell me how it came this night
    That I sleeping here was found
    With these mortals on the ground.

Exeunt. Sleepers lie still
Wind horns. Enter Theseus, Egeus, Hippolyta, and all his
train

THESEUS Go, one of you, find out the forester,
    For now our observation is performed;
    And since we have the vaward of the day,
    My love shall hear the music of my hounds.

Uncouple in the western valley, let them go;
Dispatch, I say, and find the forester.

[*Exit an Attendant*]

We will, fair queen, up to the mountain's top
And mark the musical confusion
Of hounds and echo in conjunction.

HIPPOLYTA I was with Hercules and Cadmus once,
When in a wood of Crete they bayed the bear
With hounds of Sparta; never did I hear
Such gallant chiding, for besides the groves,
The skies, the fountains, every region near
Seemed all one mutual cry. I never heard
So musical a discord, such sweet thunder.

THESEUS My hounds are bred out of the Spartan kind,
So flewed, so sanded, and their heads are hung
With ears that sweep away the morning dew,
Crook-kneed and dewlapped like Thessalian bulls,
Slow in pursuit, but matched in mouth like bells,
Each under each. A cry more tuneable
Was never hallowed to, nor cheered with horn,
In Crete, in Sparta, nor in Thessaly;
Judge when you hear. But, soft! What nymphs are
    these?

EGEUS My lord, this is my daughter here asleep,
And this, Lysander, this Demetrius is,
This Helena, old Nedar's Helena.
I wonder of their being here together.

THESEUS No doubt they rose up early to observe
    The rite of May, and hearing our intent,
    Came here in grace of our solemnity.
    But speak, Egeus; is not this the day
    That Hermia should give answer of her choice?

EGEUS It is, my lord.

THESEUS Go, bid the huntsmen wake them with their
    horns.

Horns and they wake. Shout within, they all start up.
    Good morrow, friends. Saint Valentine is past.
    Begin these woodbirds but to couple now?

LYSANDER Pardon, my lord.

THESEUS I pray you all stand up.
    I know you two are rival enemies.
    How comes this gentle concord in the world,
    That hatred is so far from jealousy,
    To sleep by hate and fear no enmity?

LYSANDER My lord, I shall reply amazedly,
    Half sleep, half waking. But as yet, I swear,
    I cannot truly say how I came here.
    But, as I think — for truly would I speak,
    And now I do bethink me, so it is —
    I came with Hermia hither. Our intent
    Was to be gone from Athens, where we might be
    Without the peril of the Athenian law.

EGEUS Enough, enough, my lord. You have enough;
    I beg the law, the law, upon his head.—
    They would have stolen away, they would, Demetrius,

Thereby to have defeated you and me:
You of your wife and me of my consent,
Of my consent that she should be your wife.

DEMETRIUS My lord, fair Helen told me of their stealth,
Of this their purpose hither to this wood,
And I in fury hither followed them;
Fair Helena in fancy followed me.
But, my good lord, I wot not by what power —
But by some power it is — my love to Hermia,
Melted as the snow, seems to me now
As the remembrance of an idle gaud
Which in my childhood I did dote upon.
And all the faith, the virtue of my heart,
The object and the pleasure of mine eye,
Is only Helena. To her, my lord,
Was I betrothed ere I saw Hermia:
But like a sickness did I loathe this food.
But, as in health, come to my natural taste,
Now I do wish it, love it, long for it,
And will for evermore be true to it.

THESEUS Fair lovers, you are fortunately met:
Of this discourse we shall hear more anon.
Egeus, I will overbear your will;
For in the temple, by and by with us,
These couples shall eternally be knit.
And, for the morning now is something worn,
Our purposed hunting shall be set aside.
Away with us to Athens; three and three,

We'll hold a feast in great solemnity.—
Come, Hippolyta.

Exeunt Duke and lords [and Hippolyta]

DEMETRIUS These things seem small and
    undistinguishable,
Like far-off mountains turnèd into clouds.

HERMIA Methinks I see these things with parted eye,
When everything seems double.

HELENA So methinks:
And I have found Demetrius like a jewel,
Mine own and not mine own.

DEMETRIUS It seems to me
That yet we sleep, we dream. Do not you think
The duke was here, and bid us follow him?

HERMIA Yea, and my father.

HELENA And Hippolyta.

LYSANDER And he bid us follow to the temple.

DEMETRIUS Why, then, we are awake; let's follow him
And by the way let us recount our dreams.

Exeunt lovers
Bottom wakes

BOTTOM When my cue comes, call me, and I will
answer. My next is, 'Most fair Pyramus.' Hey-ho!
Peter Quince? Flute, the bellows-mender? Snout, the
tinker? Starveling? God's my life, stolen hence and
left me asleep! I have had a most rare vision. I had a
dream, past the wit of man to say what dream it was.

Man is but an ass, if he go about to expound this dream. Methought I was — there is no man can tell what. Methought I was — and methought I had — but man is but a patched fool if he will offer to say what methought I had. The eye of man hath not heard, the ear of man hath not seen, man's hand is not able to taste, his tongue to conceive, nor his heart to report, what my dream was. I will get Peter Quince to write a ballad of this dream: it shall be called 'Bottom's Dream', because it hath no bottom; and I will sing it in the latter end of a play, before the duke. Peradventure, to make it the more gracious, I shall sing it at her death.   *Exit*

[Act 4 Scene 2]   *running scene 6*

Enter Quince, Flute, Snout and Starveling

QUINCE Have you sent to Bottom's house? Is he come home yet?

STARVELING He cannot be heard of. Out of doubt he is transported.

FLUTE If he come not, then the play is marred. It goes not forward, doth it?

QUINCE It is not possible: you have not a man in all Athens able to discharge Pyramus but he.

FLUTE No, he hath simply the best wit of any handicraft man in Athens.

QUINCE Yea, and the best person too, and he is a very paramour for a sweet voice.

FLUTE You must say 'paragon'. A paramour is, God bless us, a thing of naught.

Enter Snug the joiner

SNUG Masters, the duke is coming from the temple, and there is two or three lords and ladies more married. If our sport had gone forward, we had all been made men.

FLUTE O sweet bully Bottom! Thus hath he lost sixpence a day during his life; he could not have scaped sixpence a day. An the duke had not given him sixpence a day for playing Pyramus, I'll be hanged. He would have deserved it. Sixpence a day in Pyramus, or nothing.

Enter Bottom

BOTTOM Where are these lads? Where are these hearts?

QUINCE Bottom! O most courageous day! O most happy hour!

BOTTOM Masters, I am to discourse wonders: but ask me not what, for if I tell you, I am no true Athenian. I will tell you everything as it fell out.

QUINCE Let us hear, sweet Bottom.

BOTTOM Not a word of me. All that I will tell you is that the duke hath dined. Get your apparel together, good strings to your beards, new ribbons to your pumps. Meet presently at the palace, every man look o'er his part, for the short and the long is, our play is preferred. In any case, let Thisbe have clean linen, and let not him that plays the lion pare his nails, for they shall hang out for the lion's claws. And, most dear actors, eat no onions nor garlic, for we are to utter sweet breath, and I do not doubt but to hear them say, it is a sweet comedy. No more words: away! Go, away!   *Exeunt*

Act 5 Scene 1   *running scene 7*

Enter Theseus, Hippolyta, Egeus, and his lords

HIPPOLYTA 'Tis strange, my Theseus, that these lovers
    speak of.
THESEUS More strange than true. I never may believe
    These antic fables, nor these fairy toys.
    Lovers and madmen have such seething brains,
    Such shaping fantasies that apprehend
    More than cool reason ever comprehends.
    The lunatic, the lover and the poet
    Are of imagination all compact.
    One sees more devils than vast hell can hold;
    That is the madman. The lover, all as frantic,
    Sees Helen's beauty in a brow of Egypt.
    The poet's eye, in a fine frenzy rolling,
    Doth glance from heaven to earth, from earth to
      heaven,
    And as imagination bodies forth

The forms of things unknown, the poet's pen
Turns them to shapes and gives to airy nothing
A local habitation and a name.
Such tricks hath strong imagination,
That if it would but apprehend some joy,
It comprehends some bringer of that joy.
Or in the night, imagining some fear,
How easy is a bush supposed a bear!

HIPPOLYTA But all the story of the night told over,
And all their minds transfigured so together,
More witnesseth than fancy's images
And grows to something of great constancy;
But howsoever, strange and admirable.

Enter lovers: Lysander, Demetrius, Hermia, Helena

THESEUS Here come the lovers, full of joy and mirth.
Joy, gentle friends! Joy and fresh days of love
Accompany your hearts!

LYSANDER More than to us
Wait in your royal walks, your board, your bed!

THESEUS Come now, what masques, what dances shall
we have,
To wear away this long age of three hours
Between our after-supper and bedtime?
Where is our usual manager of mirth?
What revels are in hand? Is there no play
To ease the anguish of a torturing hour?
Call Egeus.

EGEUS Here, mighty Theseus.

THESEUS Say, what abridgement have you for this
    evening?
  What masque? What music? How shall we beguile
  The lazy time, if not with some delight?

EGEUS There is a brief how many sports are ripe:
  Make choice of which your highness will see first.

LYSANDER 'The battle with the Centaurs, to be sung
  By an Athenian eunuch to the harp.'

THESEUS We'll none of that. That have I told my love,
  In glory of my kinsman Hercules.

LYSANDER 'The riot of the tipsy Bacchanals,
  Tearing the Thracian singer in their rage.'

THESEUS That is an old device, and it was played
  When I from Thebes came last a conqueror.

LYSANDER 'The thrice three Muses mourning for the
    death
  Of learning, late deceased in beggary.'

THESEUS That is some satire, keen and critical,
  Not sorting with a nuptial ceremony.

LYSANDER 'A tedious brief scene of young Pyramus
  And his love Thisbe; very tragical mirth.'

THESEUS Merry and tragical? Tedious and brief?
  That is, hot ice and wondrous strange snow.
  How shall we find the concord of this discord?

EGEUS A play there is, my lord, some ten words long,
  Which is as brief as I have known a play;
  But by ten words, my lord, it is too long,
  Which makes it tedious. For in all the play

There is not one word apt, one player fitted.
And tragical, my noble lord, it is,
For Pyramus therein doth kill himself.
Which, when I saw rehearsed, I must confess,
Made mine eyes water, but more merry tears
The passion of loud laughter never shed.

THESEUS What are they that do play it?

EGEUS Hard-handed men that work in Athens here,
Which never laboured in their minds till now;
And now have toiled their unbreathed memories
With this same play, against your nuptial.

THESEUS And we will hear it.

EGEUS No, my noble lord,
It is not for you. I have heard it over,
And it is nothing, nothing in the world;
Unless you can find sport in their intents,
Extremely stretched and conned with cruel pain,
To do you service.

THESEUS I will hear that play.
For never anything can be amiss,
When simpleness and duty tender it.
Go, bring them in.— And take your places, ladies.

[Exit Egeus]

HIPPOLYTA I love not to see wretchedness o'er-charged
And duty in his service perishing.

THESEUS Why, gentle sweet, you shall see no such thing.

HIPPOLYTA He says they can do nothing in this kind.

THESEUS   The kinder we, to give them thanks for nothing.
       Our sport shall be to take what they mistake;
       And what poor duty cannot do, noble respect
       Takes it in might, not merit.
       Where I have come, great clerks have purposèd
       To greet me with premeditated welcomes;
       Where I have seen them shiver and look pale,
       Make periods in the midst of sentences,
       Throttle their practised accent in their fears,
       And in conclusion dumbly have broke off,
       Not paying me a welcome. Trust me, sweet,
       Out of this silence yet I picked a welcome.
       And in the modesty of fearful duty
       I read as much as from the rattling tongue
       Of saucy and audacious eloquence.
       Love, therefore, and tongue-tied simplicity
       In least speak most, to my capacity.

[Enter Egeus]

EGEUS   So please your grace, the Prologue is addressed.

THESEUS   Let him approach.   *Flourish [of] trumpets*

Enter the Prologue: Quince

PROLOGUE [QUINCE]   If we offend, it is with our good will.
       That you should think, we come not to offend,
       But with good will. To show our simple skill,
       That is the true beginning of our end.
       Consider then, we come but in despite.
       We do not come as minding to content you,
       Our true intent is. All for your delight

We are not here. That you should here repent you,
The actors are at hand; and by their show,
You shall know all that you are like to know.

THESEUS This fellow doth not stand upon points.

LYSANDER He hath rid his prologue like a rough colt: he
knows not the stop. A good moral, my lord. It is not
enough to speak, but to speak true.

HIPPOLYTA Indeed he hath played on his prologue like a
child on a recorder: a sound, but not in government.

THESEUS His speech was like a tangled chain: nothing
impaired, but all disordered. Who is next?

*Enter, with a trumpet[er] before them, Pyramus [Bottom]
and Thisbe [Flute], Wall [Snout], Moonshine [Starveling]
and Lion [Snug]*

PROLOGUE [QUINCE] Gentles, perchance you wonder at
this show,
But wonder on, till truth make all things plain.
This man is Pyramus, if you would know;
This beauteous lady Thisbe is certain.
This man with lime and rough-cast doth present
Wall, that vile Wall which did these lovers sunder.
And through Wall's chink, poor souls, they are content
To whisper. At the which let no man wonder.
This man, with lantern, dog, and bush of thorn,
Presenteth Moonshine. For, if you will know,
By moonshine did these lovers think no scorn
To meet at Ninus' tomb, there, there to woo.
This grisly beast, which Lion hight by name,

The trusty Thisbe, coming first by night,
Did scare away, or rather did affright.
And as she fled, her mantle she did fall,
Which Lion vile with bloody mouth did stain.
Anon comes Pyramus, sweet youth and tall,
And finds his trusty Thisbe's mantle slain;
Whereat, with blade, with bloody blameful blade,
He bravely broached his boiling bloody breast.
And Thisbe, tarrying in mulberry shade,
His dagger drew, and died. For all the rest,
Let Lion, Moonshine, Wall, and lovers twain
At large discourse, while here they do remain.

Exeunt all but Wall

THESEUS I wonder if the lion be to speak.

DEMETRIUS No wonder, my lord: one lion may, when
many asses do.

WALL [SNOUT] In this same interlude it doth befall
That I, one Snout by name, present a wall.
And such a wall, as I would have you think,
That had in it a crannied hole or chink,
Through which the lovers, Pyramus and Thisbe,
Did whisper often, very secretly.
This loam, this rough-cast and this stone doth show
That I am that same wall; the truth is so.
And this the cranny is, right and sinister,
Through which the fearful lovers are to whisper.

THESEUS Would you desire lime and hair to speak
better?

DEMETRIUS It is the wittiest partition that ever I heard
　　discourse, my lord.

THESEUS Pyramus draws near the wall. Silence!

Enter Pyramus

PYRAMUS [BOTTOM] O grim-looked night! O night with
　　hue so black!

　　O night, which ever art when day is not!

　　O night, O night! Alack, alack, alack,

　　I fear my Thisbe's promise is forgot.

　　And thou, O wall, thou sweet and lovely wall

　　That stands between her father's ground and mine!

　　Thou wall, O wall, O sweet and lovely wall,

　　Show me thy chink, to blink through with mine
　　　eyne!

　　Thanks, courteous wall. Jove shield thee well for
　　　this.

　　But what see I? No Thisbe do I see.

　　O wicked wall, through whom I see no bliss!

　　Cursed be thy stones for thus deceiving me!

THESEUS The wall, methinks, being sensible, should
　　curse again.

PYRAMUS [BOTTOM] No, in truth, sir, he should not.
　　'Deceiving me' is Thisbe's cue; she is to enter and I
　　am to spy her through the wall. You shall see, it will
　　fall pat as I told you. Yonder she comes.

Enter Thisbe

THISBE [FLUTE] O wall, full often hast thou heard my
　　moans,

For parting my fair Pyramus and me.
My cherry lips have often kissed thy stones,
Thy stones with lime and hair knit up in thee.

PYRAMUS [BOTTOM] I see a voice; now will I to the chink,
To spy an I can hear my Thisbe's face. Thisbe?

THISBE [FLUTE] My love thou art, my love I think.

PYRAMUS [BOTTOM] Think what thou wilt, I am thy
lover's grace
And like Limander am I trusty still.

THISBE [FLUTE] And I like Helen, till the Fates me kill.

PYRAMUS [BOTTOM] Not Shafalus to Procrus was so true.

THISBE [FLUTE] As Shafalus to Procrus, I to you.

PYRAMUS [BOTTOM] O, kiss me through the hole of
this vile wall!

THISBE [FLUTE] I kiss the wall's hole, not your lips at all.

PYRAMUS [BOTTOM] Wilt thou at Ninny's tomb meet
me straightway?

THISBE [FLUTE] 'Tide life, 'tide death, I come without
delay.   [*Exeunt Pyramus and Thisbe*]

WALL [SNOUT] Thus have I, Wall, my part dischargèd so;
And, being done, thus Wall away doth go.   *Exit*

THESEUS Now is the mural down between the two
neighbours.

DEMETRIUS No remedy, my lord, when walls are so
wilful to hear without warning.

HIPPOLYTA This is the silliest stuff that e'er I heard.

THESEUS The best in this kind are but shadows, and the
worst are no worse, if imagination amend them.

HIPPOLYTA It must be your imagination then, and not theirs.

THESEUS If we imagine no worse of them than they of themselves, they may pass for excellent men. Here come two noble beasts in, a man and a lion.

Enter Lion and Moonshine [*with a lantern, thorn-bush and dog*]

LION [SNUG] You, ladies, you, whose gentle hearts do fear
The smallest monstrous mouse that creeps on floor,
May now perchance both quake and tremble here,
When lion rough in wildest rage doth roar.
Then know that I, one Snug the joiner, am
A lion fell, nor else no lion's dam,
For if I should as lion come in strife
Into this place, 'twere pity on my life.

THESEUS A very gentle beast, and of a good conscience.

DEMETRIUS The very best at a beast, my lord, that e'er I saw.

LYSANDER This lion is a very fox for his valour.

THESEUS True, and a goose for his discretion.

DEMETRIUS Not so, my lord, for his valour cannot carry his discretion, and the fox carries the goose.

THESEUS His discretion, I am sure, cannot carry his valour, for the goose carries not the fox. It is well. Leave it to his discretion, and let us hearken to the moon.

MOONSHINE [STARVELING] This lantern doth the hornèd moon present—

DEMETRIUS He should have worn the horns on his head.

THESEUS He is no crescent, and his horns are invisible within the circumference.

MOONSHINE [STARVELING] This lantern doth the hornèd moon present:

Myself the man i'th'moon doth seem to be.

THESEUS This is the greatest error of all the rest; the man should be put into the lantern. How is it else the man i'th'moon?

DEMETRIUS He dares not come there for the candle. For you see it is already in snuff.

HIPPOLYTA I am aweary of this moon; would he would change!

THESEUS It appears, by his small light of discretion, that he is in the wane. But yet, in courtesy, in all reason, we must stay the time.

LYSANDER Proceed, Moon.

MOONSHINE [STARVELING] All that I have to say is to tell you that the lantern is the moon; I, the man in the moon; this thorn-bush, my thorn-bush; and this dog, my dog.

DEMETRIUS Why, all these should be in the lantern, for they are in the moon. But silence — here comes Thisbe.

Enter Thisbe

THISBE [FLUTE] This is old Ninny's tomb. Where is my love?

LION [SNUG] O!

The lion roars. Thisbe runs off [*dropping her mantle*]

DEMETRIUS Well roared, Lion.

THESEUS Well run, Thisbe.

HIPPOLYTA Well shone, Moon. Truly, the moon shines
    with a good grace.

                [*Lion shakes Thisbe's mantle, and exits*]

THESEUS Well moused, Lion.

DEMETRIUS And then came Pyramus.

LYSANDER And so the lion vanished.

Enter Pyramus

PYRAMUS [BOTTOM] Sweet Moon, I thank thee for thy
    sunny beams,

  I thank thee, Moon, for shining now so bright,

  For by thy gracious, golden, glittering gleams,

  I trust to taste of truest Thisbe sight.

        But stay, O spite!

        But mark, poor knight,

        What dreadful dole is here?

        Eyes, do you see?

        How can it be?

        O dainty duck! O dear!

        Thy mantle good,

        What, stained with blood!

        Approach, you Furies fell!

        O Fates, come, come,

        Cut thread and thrum,

        Quail, crush, conclude, and quell!

THESEUS This passion, and the death of a dear friend,
would go near to make a man look sad.

HIPPOLYTA Beshrew my heart, but I pity the man.

PYRAMUS [BOTTOM] O wherefore, Nature, didst thou
lions frame?
Since lion vile hath here deflowered my dear:
Which is — no, no — which was the fairest dame
That lived, that loved, that liked, that looked
with cheer.
Come, tears, confound:
Out, sword, and wound
The pap of Pyramus,
Ay, that left pap,
Where heart doth hop:
Thus die I, thus, thus, thus.
Now am I dead,
Now am I fled,
My soul is in the sky.
Tongue, lose thy light,
Moon take thy flight,   [*Exit Moonshine*]
Now die, die, die, die, die.

DEMETRIUS No die, but an ace for him; for he is but one.

LYSANDER Less than an ace, man: for he is dead, he is
nothing.

THESEUS With the help of a surgeon he might yet
recover, and prove an ass.

HIPPOLYTA How chance Moonshine is gone before
Thisbe comes back and finds her lover?

Enter Thisbe

THESEUS She will find him by starlight. Here she comes,
and her passion ends the play.

HIPPOLYTA Methinks she should not use a long one for
such a Pyramus: I hope she will be brief.

DEMETRIUS A mote will turn the balance, which
Pyramus, which Thisbe, is the better.

LYSANDER She hath spied him already with those sweet
eyes.

DEMETRIUS And thus she means, *videlicet*—

THISBE [FLUTE] Asleep, my love?
　　　　　　　What, dead, my dove?
　　　　　　　O Pyramus, arise!
　　　　　　　Speak, speak. Quite dumb?
　　　　　　　Dead, dead? A tomb
　　　　　　　Must cover thy sweet eyes.
　　　　　　　These lily lips,
　　　　　　　This cherry nose,
　　　　　　　These yellow cowslip cheeks,
　　　　　　　Are gone, are gone!
　　　　　　　Lovers, make moan:
　　　　　　　His eyes were green as leeks.
　　　　　　　O Sisters Three,
　　　　　　　Come, come to me,
　　　　　　　With hands as pale as milk.
　　　　　　　Lay them in gore,
　　　　　　　Since you have shore
　　　　　　　With shears his thread of silk.

Tongue, not a word.
Come, trusty sword,
Come, blade, my breast imbrue.
And farewell friends,
Thus Thisbe ends:
Adieu, adieu, adieu.

THESEUS Moonshine and Lion are left to bury the dead.

DEMETRIUS Ay, and Wall too.

BOTTOM No, I assure you, the wall is down that parted their fathers. Will it please you to see the epilogue, or to hear a Bergamasque dance between two of our company?

THESEUS No epilogue, I pray you, for your play needs no excuse. Never excuse; for when the players are all dead, there need none to be blamed. Marry, if he that writ it had played Pyramus and hung himself in Thisbe's garter, it would have been a fine tragedy: and so it is, truly, and very notably discharged. But come, your Bergamasque; let your epilogue alone.
The iron tongue of midnight hath told twelve.
Lovers, to bed, 'tis almost fairy time.
I fear we shall out-sleep the coming morn
As much as we this night have overwatched.
This palpable-gross play hath well beguiled
The heavy gait of night. Sweet friends, to bed.
A fortnight hold we this solemnity,
In nightly revels and new jollity.   *Exeunt*

Enter [Robin] Puck

ROBIN Now the hungry lion roars,
  And the wolf beholds the moon.
  Whilst the heavy ploughman snores,
  All with weary task fordone.
  Now the wasted brands do glow,
  Whilst the screech-owl, screeching loud,
  Puts the wretch that lies in woe
  In remembrance of a shroud.
  Now it is the time of night
  That the graves all gaping wide,
  Every one lets forth his sprite,
  In the church-way paths to glide.
  And we fairies that do run
  By the triple Hecate's team,
  From the presence of the sun,
  Following darkness like a dream,
  Now are frolic; not a mouse
  Shall disturb this hallowed house.
  I am sent with broom before,
  To sweep the dust behind the door.

Enter King and Queen of Fairies [*Oberon and Titania*]
with their train

OBERON Through the house give glimmering light,
  By the dead and drowsy fire,
  Every elf and fairy sprite
  Hop as light as bird from briar,
  And this ditty, after me,
  Sing, and dance it trippingly.

TITANIA First, rehearse this song by rote,
    To each word a warbling note.
    Hand in hand, with fairy grace,
    Will we sing and bless this place.
[**FAIRIES** *sing*]   *The Song*
        Now until the break of day
        Through this house each fairy stray.
        To the best bride-bed will we,
        Which by us shall blessèd be.
        And the issue there create
        Ever shall be fortunate.
        So shall all the couples three
        Ever true in loving be.
        And the blots of Nature's hand
        Shall not in their issue stand.
        Never mole, hare-lip, nor scar,
        Nor mark prodigious, such as are
        Despisèd in nativity,
        Shall upon their children be.
        With this field-dew consecrate,
        Every fairy take his gait,
        And each several chamber bless,
        Through this palace, with sweet peace.
        Ever shall in safety rest,
        And the owner of it blest.
        Trip away, make no stay;
        Meet me all by break of day.
                    [*Exeunt all but Robin*]

ROBIN If we shadows have offended,
    Think but this, and all is mended,
    That you have but slumbered here
    While these visions did appear.
    And this weak and idle theme,
    No more yielding but a dream,
    Gentles, do not reprehend.
    If you pardon, we will mend.
    And, as I am an honest Puck,
    If we have unearnèd luck
    Now to scape the serpent's tongue,
    We will make amends ere long:
    Else the Puck a liar call.
    So, goodnight unto you all.
    Give me your hands, if we be friends,
    And Robin shall restore amends.